THE BUSINESS OF
YOU

The Life You Crave

THE BUSINESS OF
YOU

APRIL B. JONES

The Business of YOU

Copyright © 2017 by April B. Jones

All rights reserved.

Publisher:
April B. Jones
KAB Enterprises, LLC
www.aprilbjones.com

Publishing consultant:
Professional Woman Publishing, LLC
www.pwnbooks.com

ISBN: 978-0-578-19176-8

Disclaimer:
The information contained in this book is based upon the author's experience, knowledge, and opinion. The author and publisher will not be held liable for the use or misuse of the information in this book.

This book is lovingly dedicated to my mother,
Shirley Gene Hill Thomas (1948 - 2016)

She shared in all my joys and sorrows, my trials, failures, and achievements; and whose unfaltering love, courage and devotion have been the strength of my striving.

Contents

Acknowledgements	1
Introduction	3
Chapter 1 How to Define Your Dreams and put them into Action	5
Chapter 2 Creating Success	21
Chapter 3 Balancing Your Home Business and Family Life	35
Chapter 4 Comfortably Confident	49
Chapter 5 Overcoming Setbacks	59
Chapter 6 Learning Knows No Age Limit	69
Chapter 7 Coping and Control: Managing Stress	79
Chapter 8 Finding Your Truth	91
Chapter 9 Devise a Plan and Get On With It	101
An Invitation from April	111
About the Author	115

Acknowledgements

I wholeheartedly thank Professional Woman Publishing for making this book possible, and especially Linda Ellis Eastman for her invaluable editorial expertise.

To you, the holder and reader of this book; I offer these tools to help you in your pursuit of The Life You Crave. May success attend your quest!

To my son, Graylin R. Walker, II, thank you for being my reason and motivation. For always believing in me and my promises to you. I'm so extremely honored that you are my son and grateful to also call you my friend.

Heartfelt thanks to some wonderful and supportive friends: Roschelle Mack Baustista, Laryssa Dickerson Somerville, Doris Ridley Holder, Valora Reid Bishop, Delisa Robinson Suggs, Sandranette Moses, and Tina Marie Harrison.

To my family, Donna Hill Boyd, Brenda Lyles Adams, Cynthia Adams McDonald, Michelle Hill, Stephanie Boggs and Adrienne Wilson Jones, as those like family, Saundra Holt and Laura Woodland, for your presence and unwavering love and support during my darkest hour and the many hours that followed when my mother went home to glory.

Special thanks to my clients and the many participants from my workshops, private coaching sessions, and consultations for letting me into your life. Good for you, for making a committed effort to turning your life's vision into a reality.

Finally, Joice Hill Nieffer, the very first person to read this book. Thank you for support, as it was much appreciated.

To my husband Kendyll, thank you. He afforded me the opportunity to share my thoughts and views with him endlessly while providing constant supportive feedback. His love, devotion, encouragement, and support of me "Living the Life I Crave", have allowed me to become who I am today, and I love him so very much for that!

Introduction

We all have a vision for our life visions and dreams. Visions of attending or returning to college and obtaining a degree, being comfortable in our own skin, balancing our home business and family life, overcoming barriers, or living an overall successful life. Unfortunately, for most of us, these dreams seldom come true.

Sometimes, this is because our circumstances make it impossible for us to live the life we want. But more likely than not, we simply don't organize or apply ourselves appropriately. We don't know where to start, or how to turn our visions and dreams into reality. Then one day, we wake up to find that life has passed us by.

Let's face it, many of us often spend more time planning a vacation or a wedding than we do planning our life and career.

This is a tragedy. Once we reach a certain age, we look back on where we are in life, what we've accomplished as well as what we never accomplished and why life has never seemed satisfying. It also means that we could reach retirement age thinking about the various opportunities that we missed, and relive the woulda, coulda, shouldas.

The great news for you – this does not have to be your future. With a little preparation and due diligence, whether you are a recent college grad, a mid-level Federal employee, an empty nester, a stay at home mom returning to the workforce, or a retiree, you can map out and exciting future.

When we have a vision for our lives it makes everything easier, from goal-setting, prioritizing actions and day-to-day activities, to making tough and life altering decisions. In addition, when our goals align with our visions and dreams we have for our life – and what's most important to us – we're more motivated.

Where to start?

Many of you may already have specific goals in mind. But to achieve our goals we need to find ways (in these busy lives of ours) to stay energized, keep moving forward and getting things done. In this book are tools to help you do just that – to identify your dreams, clarify your vision, achieve your goals, keep moving forward, and find the energy you'll need to stay the course.

It will be a process to take your overarching vision and then chunk that vision down into smaller, more meaningful goals with which to move forward. This book was written as an inspiration guide with visioning exercises to help you envision and set the scene for the next big thing in your life, as well as providing essential input to keep you motivated and moving forward.

After reading this book and completing the exercises, you will feel energized by spending more time with people who inspire and support you and doing both more of what you love – and less of what you don't! You will also be more effective as you plan your months and weeks ahead and create some unique supportive habits to help you be more successful living the life you dream and envision.

Finally, I want to congratulate you for starting your journey to turning your life's vision into a reality. Even if you are just trying to get an idea of where to start, you are going to benefit from the content of this book because you can use what you learn to make changes in your own life or help someone else make changes in theirs.

CHAPTER ONE

How to Define Your Dreams and put them into Action

Another New Year will be here before you know it. I know what you're thinking "New Year? That's way off." You know what, email me January 2nd and feel free to tell me that the time between now and the New Year dragged on. When was the last New Year's Eve when you DIDN'T think "boy, I can't believe that year flew by"?

So yes, the big moment is coming. You know the one when the clock strikes twelve. That yearly period when people resolve to make wishful (and too often ironic) resolutions. The point where we head back into our default state: resignation.

We're consummate professionals of being able to dream the dream. But then we all know what transpires. Our dreams dissipate with a cartoon-like pop. Even though they're fresh in our minds, like the carrot on a stick, they're always slightly out of reach.

As it turns out, while it takes some courage to dream, it takes an even greater amount of resources and will power to actually make it a reality.

If making your dreams come true were easy, everyone would do it. You have to define it ... own it ... and then stick with it.

Dreams are meaningless if we don't take that first step towards acting on them. The most difficult step of any journey is the first one.

Let's see how this critical step is accomplished.

How to define your dream (Without using Webster's)

Sure it's fashionable to mumble about your dream while tossing in a handful of way over-used jargon. But there's a slight problem. It doesn't get you any closer to achieving the dream. OK, so it's more of a big problem. That was just some sarcasm tossed in for affect. Hopefully the desired effect was accomplished.

It's important to be crystal clear about what you want; at least to yourself. After all, if there is anybody you don't want to lie to, it's yourself. You'd find out the truth eventually anyway.

It's surprisingly difficult for people to articulate exactly what their dream looks like. Which, as I said at the beginning of this section, really puts a damper on actually achieving the dream.

Let's try a quick exercise, shall we?

FIRST   Close your eyes and visualize yourself living the dream. What about it attracts you the most? Be specific. Extremely specific. Now explain your dream, but pretend you're describing it to a three-year old.

SECOND   Be as specific as possible.

Specific sounds like: "I want to become a sensitive, well-trained journalist, who impacts teens".

Not at all specific sounds like: "I want to become famous" or "I want to make an impact".

THIRD   Is it your dream or someone else's? This is a game-changing question. If you find a career appealing only because it means sitting in the same classes as your friends or because your mother decided it for you, it becomes their dream, not yours. Nothing here applies if it is someone else's dream and not yours. Sorry. In more ways than one.

Some questions to help hone in on your dream:

- What do I love doing? Truly love. (Nothing illegal please.)
- What did I love doing as a child? What kind of a life would allow me to recapture that feeling?
- If I had a million dollars, would I still do it anyway?

Use stepping stones not leaping stones

If we think about the gap between where we are and where we want to be, we feel overwhelmed. Well, one option is simply not to think about it. Which is a horrible option. A better option is to take on the task piecemeal. Rome wasn't built in a day. Nobody wrote a best-selling murder mystery novel overnight. The way you conquer big objectives is to break down your ultimate goal into smaller, less anxiety generating steps.

Visualization Part 1. Close your eyes and visualize a staircase. Now imagine with your dream or goal at the top. Picture the first step. It's just one up from the landing. Now assign a very simple task needed to reach your goal to this step. On the stair above it, assign the next small task needed to propel you closer to the goal. Now just keep visualizing these steps until you've reached the top of the staircase (i.e. your dream). See how easy? Just make sure these steps are simple and manageable.

The staircase shouldn't be 2 or 3 steps high. Make sure the steps are very specific to the final goal. (Step 1 to writing a novel could be "think of a title" and Step 2, "map out the plot" and so on).

Visualization Part 2. Want to make this more fun? (and therefore more likely to accomplish)? Reward yourself when you finish each step, even if it's with just a cupcake. Who doesn't love cupcakes? Oh, not you? No problem, any small reward will do. Every small step is progress, whether you acknowledge it or not.

Kill the Dream-Killers

OK, not literally, just remove them. You are super excited about your new plan, but as always, there are people dampening your spirits. I place critical people into two camps. One camp are individuals that actually have something constructive to say. This is usually the smaller camp. OK, it's tiny. But this is a camp that I listen to.

The other camp are people with just a bunch of aimless negativity. I tune these people out like the annoying guy at a party. I try to surround myself with people who genuinely want the best for me and are rooting for me. I suggest you do the same. That's the only way you can move your goals from the "dreaming about it" file to the "taking action" file.

Picture yourself taking your car out for a ride on a beautiful day. Who are the people making sure you're heading in the right direction? You guessed it, they are the people who want the best for you. Now, who are the people twiddling their thumbs, the ones just along for a ride? Their main function is to add dead weight. Last, who are the ones piling on rocks and suitcases of bitterness to the already occupied vehicle. That's worse than dead weight. It's dead weight times ten.

Don't be afraid, point out the people in your life who are toxic and drain of your energy. It's ok, you can do it silently, and no one must know you are pointing them out. Now that we have the enemy targeted, slowly step away from them. It might seem mean-spirited and impossible, but you'll be surprised by how clear and rejuvenated you feel in the absence of all of that unnecessary drama. You want reality, not reality TV.

But don't confuse this group with another group. The group who might say things or give you opinions that you may not like, but are trying to help you and not hinder you. It goes without saying that these people are not dream-killers. They have your best interests at heart. Take what they say into account, but don't take it as sacred. Listen to your intuition when deciding whether to follow their advice.

How bad do you want it?

People of the world are constantly seeking out quick, sure-fire recipe to success. Magic weight loss pills. Get rich quick courses. The lottery. Do any really work? That was a rhetorical question, you already know the answer. There is one super important key ingredient: you need to really, really, want it. That's the real secret. That's the difference between people who get what they want and people who don't.

An aspiring designer could apply to 100 design schools and be rejected by everyone to which she applied. She could choose to pack in her dream at that point or she could get more real-world experience and apply again. A best-selling author could wait to become rich so she had time to write her novel or she could hold down two other jobs to support her craft. It's about perseverance. Like the ace researcher who goes through months of fine-tuning the exact questionnaires or methodology. Or the girl with an amazing voice who is a mother of two, but still manages to record a demo and pop it in the mailbox; wanting to make the best of two distinctive worlds. Do you see a pattern here?

You need to want something so much that you still want it, even when it doesn't fall on your lap.

Are you doing one or all of the following steps to achieve your goal?

1. You are learning everything you can about your dream. You are diving in to the details headfirst. From the most obvious particulars, to the more uninteresting facts. Do you know your dream inside-out? And outside in? Try this: Every time you come across anything related to each step of your dream, tack it to your wall or pin it to your corkboard.

2. You read books or biographies about other people that became successful in the field you have your eye on. Notice how I said became, because people aren't born successful, it takes work. A lot of work. Are you making notes to get inspired? Analyze what worked and didn't work for them. Use this information to determine what will work and what will not work for you.

3. Like above, are you listening to podcast or following blogs? There are podcasts and blogs about every profession and hobby known to man. Subscribe to a couple. Hang out in the forums. You will find that as you take in more information and become part of that online community, the task ahead will not seem so daunting. If they can do it, so can you.

Awaken your mind!

Some people sleep seven or eight hours a night, others sleep for months, even years at a time. I don't mean the kind you do in bed; I mean walking around with an indifferent mind. If your mind's asleep, frustrated and dismissive, it's extremely difficult to get to where you want to be. In the same vein, when your mind's awake and energized, nothing seems unachievable. Ironically, this is the easiest and yet the toughest part for most people. If you don't understand that logic, maybe your mind is asleep. Here are two ways to help wake it up:

1. Live healthy. Eat, sleep and exercise right. So simple a child can do it. Yet few actually keep this regiment. Forty-five percent of Americans say that poor or insufficient sleep affected their daily activities at least once in the past seven days. Want proof that better sleep works? Try a simple experiment, get two or three hours' less sleep than you need one night. The next night, add back the two or three hours. You tell me which day after you felt more present and focused. While nobody says you have to put in Olympic athlete hours at the gym, walking to the bus stop after your stop or walking short distances alone goes a long way in reducing your anxiety and enhancing your thinking.

2. Make a vision board. Which is, a "board" that encapsulates your "vision." Take out old magazines and newspapers, and follow your instinct in cutting out pictures that represent your vision. Then put them on a board. Once that's done, hang it in your bedroom. I promise, you'll be surprised at what a difference it makes.

Expel distractions!

Ok, so now you're nice and well rested and your mind is awake. Time to attract what you need. Now expelling distractions shouldn't be too hard. The object is to bring in more of what helps you to get working and dreaming, and less of what distracts you. Here are two key points:

1. Fool your brain. Your mind is smart, but not so smart it can't be tricked. It really doesn't know the difference between thinking and doing. So one simple technique is to use positive, present tense ("I'm an amazing dancer!").

2. What's needed is what is needed. Focus on what you need to do, and not what you shouldn't do. ("I could write two scenes a day" and not, "I must not procrastinate").

3. Be like Steve. Steve Jobs was famous for his minimalism. Look at Apple products and the Apple stores. Clean. Simple. So de-clutter in every sense of the word. Unless this goes against your job description, do not check your mail more than twice a day. Streamline tasks, such as push-notifications. Maybe every ten minutes is over kill, maybe every hour is fine. That personal project you're no longer passionate about, kill it to make more time for what you want to achieve.

Good is the enemy of great

This is a rule that needs to be engraved in every wall. Settling for mediocrity inevitably leads to complacency, which pretty much kills the prospect of growth. Your work mustn't just pass the test, it must blow the test away.

1. Settling can only be temporary. Sometimes we (hopefully only occasionally), have to "settle". For instance; for financial reasons. Remember that just because your dream isn't fulfilled right away doesn't mean you need to bail on it. Dreams don't have a time constraint; just because it doesn't happen right away, doesn't mean it won't happen at all. Continue working and make decisions that move you in the direction of your goal.

2. Kill complacency. Kill it by respecting what you do. If you don't respect it, I guarantee you no one else will. OK, so some tasks are not your most favorite. Then at least devise fun and interesting ways to complete that task. Everything you do, no matter how unrelated you think it might be, gives you the skills and momentum for many

other aspects of your life; and this is especially true when you give that effort the regard it deserves. When you work mechanically (like an assembly line) kiss the value goodbye. In no time, you'll wonder who you've become and where the heck you're headed.

Nobody becomes successful by dreaming

Let me explain. Yes, you should dream, but you can't be successful by JUST dreaming. You must follow dreaming with actions. It's great to be a dreamer. We all love dreaming! But without action, nothing gets accomplished. That is the biggest difference between the achievers and the non-achievers.

So far we've broken your dream down into achievable steps and created a healthy attitude. Then we've summoned some positive energy and a great support system. Know when the perfect time to get moving is? Right now. Here are a few steps for the action phase:

Step 1 is actually 1 step – Take that first step. Ignore everything that's holding you back. Make that phone call, write that first word or press SEND on that email draft. Just do it!

Step 2 – Get a pro. Still lost? Hire a certified professional life coach (I'm available). They will help you streamline your goals, offer support and clarity to make your life work. According to International Coaching Federation, 99% of companies and individuals who've hired a professional coach are "satisfied" with the overall experience. 96% said they would repeat the process. So obviously it works.

Step 3 – Stuck in Step 2? Much of that inertia could be because you require a little more help in the technicalities. Don't be afraid to re-take a tutorial, take a refresher class or ask for help from someone who has enough experience to help you learn the ropes.

Take responsibility!

It's easy to be a Debbie downer. To say "Oh I try, but the system goes against me" or "No one supports me," "This town just doesn't have any opportunity." Woe is me! I hate to be the bearer of bad news, but only you are responsible for making your dreams come true. The days of Prince Charming whisking you away to your happily ever after are long gone (or exist only in the movies). Who wants to have to answer to Prince Charming anyway? You are in control of your behavior and you choose how to react to each situation. There's a setback? No problem, you'll figure what went wrong, and make it right. You're no damsel in distress, you're the hero. You see, there's a lot of power in being accountable for yourself. Here are some steps for this section:

1. Mind your mind. Be mindful, aware and oriented to the present. Time spent mulling over past wrongs or setbacks is time you could use to make things better.

2. Play the swap the pronoun game. Replace 'I' with 'you'. 'I' statements encourage responsibility. ("Those days, when I feel crabby, I felt …" as opposed to "You know, those days when you feel crabby and everything goes against you")

3. Employ a drill sergeant. Appoint someone to constantly check on your progress. Tell more people (when you're ready!) about your plan. This way, even when you slack off, you'll feel the need to get moving; as you've made yourself answerable to someone (or many someones).

It's important to **be open**. In the process of putting your dream into action, you might discover a newfound passion or path. Allow yourself to consider those avenues! Water is one of the most powerful elements on earth. Because it is flexible. Achieving your dreams is not about being rigid and controlled, you could, along the way, realize that your dreams have changed.

HOW TO DEFINE YOUR DREAMS

Integrate this philosophy into your journey and see how you enjoy the process more. Your perspective will widen the scope of your journey. Every time I view a failure as an experience and see continuity in starting over, I can feel my line of vision broaden. Some of my best work happens when I enjoy the process, and forget about keeping my eye on the prize.

Now that you have a solid game plan, what amazing goals will you accomplish? List them below:

1. _____

2. _____

3. _____

4. _____

5. _____

Exercise

A simple way for you to check your progress is to keep a daily journal. Besides allowing you to see yourself moving forward, it can release your hidden feelings, which does wonders to manage stress. A journal will also help you spot both negative and positive routines and patterns. Finally see what you are achieving, because most of us are so busy, we don't see what we have achieved. On the next page, I have included a sample journal template.

Journal

Date: _____

Overview of the Day:

_____

_____

Breakdown of the Day

What did I enjoy most about my day?

_____

_____

What would I like to do less of in my day?

_____

_____

What did I learn today?

_____

_____

If I could, what would I do differently?

_____

_____

Completing your journal

Overview of the Day

This is exactly what it sounds like. A simple overview of what happened during your day. You need to be aware of what is currently going on in that mind of yours. Record all your thoughts and feelings; "today I met an old friend for dinner", "I thought it was great to get out of the office and forget any problems of the morning." "I am looking forward to doing that again in the near future."

This section will record your highs and lows, your triggers and your emotions. Record any and all thoughts. It's all top of mind stuff. Record both the positives (the steps forward) as well as any negatives (steps back).

- Why did you have a good/bad day?
- Who did you meet that changed your state?
- Where were you?
- What were you saying to yourself?

Breakdown of the Day

What did I enjoy most about my day?

- Why was this part of your day good?
- What were you doing?
- What made it fun and exciting? Who were you with?
- What would you like to do more of?

What would I like to do less of in my day?

Think about what you didn't enjoy about this day. But don't think about it too much. Just imagine your day as a TV show, watching yourself on the television.

- Which part of your day did you not enjoy?
- Why did you not enjoy this?

What did I learn today?

We learn every day. Or at least we have the ability to learn every day. Sometimes we just don't recognize the learning opportunity. One of the things that drive humans forward is our quest for knowledge. Think about the things you enjoyed and the things you didn't enjoy in your day, then ask yourself for each individual item "what have I learned from this?"

Record anything you've learned about yourself; how you acted in different situations, what you enjoyed doing, how you handled problems, how others affected you, what made you laugh. Write down anything you were not originally aware of. You'd be surprised how powerful the simple act of forcing yourself to take notice is.

If I could, what would I do differently?

Sometimes we shoot from the hip, acting spontaneously. In many cases this can be a positive thing. Then there are times it's not so positive. I'm sure you know what I am talking about. We've all heard people say "in hindsight …" And we also have had times where we talk ourselves out of doing something only to later regret that decision later.

Now you've got the tools to not only define your dreams, but to put them into action. So there's no excuses, stop procrastinating and start accomplishing your goals.

Chapter Notes

CHAPTER TWO

Creating Success

"How can I be successful?" To me, there has never been a more misused and misunderstood question. We are living in a time when "success" has consumed us. It's the drug of choice for the new millennium. We can't get enough. And with this new obsession, apparently, there is no in-between: you are either successful or you're a wanna-be.

Thank the media. They happily pollute the airwaves and social media with people who have it all ... take Bill Gates, he's the genius programmer who dropped out of college and created one of the world's most important corporations on his own. See how easy it is. See how he's a guy to be looked up to and you're not? Or Jennifer Hudson, when in 2004 she came in seventh place on the third season of American Idol, but in 2006 went on to earn an Academy Award, a Golden Globe Award, a BAFTA Award, and a Screen Actors Guild Award for Best Supporting Actress for the movie Dream Girls. And then there's Kim Kardashian. A reality TV star whose life some envy, even if they are not too keen on how she got there. These are the role models our beloved media has put forward. I'm not saying they haven't accomplished things we can all envy. What is sad, however, is that we are told they are to be respected because of the material wealth they have collected. We are to adore them for working hard at something that would consume them.

The image of success we create (or more correctly have created for us) is the image after achieving great success, and everyone is there to see and clap. Unfortunately, most just want to skip to this final part of the journey.

Is this really the best model? What is success, after all? Is it some pre-defined concept?

Maybe you have been looking at it wrong all this time. Maybe the reason you don't feel that constant rush and overall sensation of wellbeing is because you're not searching in the right places. Like the old country song, you're "looking for love in all the wrong places."

Introduce yourself to yourself

There are those who know who they are and what emotional needs they have. These lucky few have come one step closer to fulfillment. Most people, however, realize at a certain point they are unhappy because they have not been doing what they were meant to. Trust me, there is something waiting out there for everyone. Maybe your calling is cooking or medicine or perhaps you're supposed to be a yogi. People fall victim to stereotypes all the time. We easily digest the preconceived ideas we are fed about the perfect life and what it should be. Some enjoy a steady diet of incarnating socially acceptable ideas. They are a faceless number, a character from Orwell's "1984", sheepishly following the crowd for no other reason than they were told to do so. In order defy Big Brother, one has to bring their soul forward, to embark on a journey of self-discovery.

Let us try a set of questions to help us realize who we are at our deepest core:

- What type of activity do I always enjoy and always resort to in my spare time?
- What has been there for me all my life?
- In which moment(s) do I feel most comfortable with myself?
- Who was I most drawn to as a child?

As cliché as it sounds, going back to one's childhood is essential for unearthing our most sincere egos. Egos in the Freudian terms, what he expressed as *"organized part of the personality structure that includes defensive, perceptual, intellectual-cognitive, and executive function."* In layman's terms, it is the decision-making component of our personality. Ideally the ego works by reason (whereas the id is chaotic and totally unreasonable.) But enough with the Freudian tangent. Childhood is the time when major traits of our personalities are being formed and when we are having experiences that will define us forever.

Do some reflecting on your youth. After this introspection, which I strongly recommend you do as often as possible, you can begin to accept who you are, and start working on what you want to improve.

No one is saying it will be easy. You must force yourself to go back (from before the process of finding of the self) to old thoughts, even though some may be painful. You must push yourself past the threshold, like an athlete pushing past the edge of pain tolerance. It is then that you will feel at peace with yourself. You will feel grounded; a sense of inner security comes from knowing who you are and what you really want. I promise you will notice changes all around you: your inner grouch won't visit as often and your crazy mood swings will give way to a nicer, calmer, more even-keeled you. Which is a great thing because these are common characteristics of successful people.

Success is different to everyone. Maybe you were raised to believe that success means working for a large corporation. Or that fame is everything. But after reflecting on success' true meaning, you discover that success is having a big, happy family or materializing that crazy business idea you've had for a long time. In the end, you realize that you don't have to have money to be rich.

Love people, not money

We all know the "successful" person who basically lives at the office. They barely spend time with their family, who feel left behind and craving their presence. But success of career does not equal success. Success is an overall feeling of achievement in all areas: work, family, hobbies, etc. People who neglect the loved ones in their lives in exchange for climbing the corporate ladder often pay a steep price in their personal life. Happy relationships are a huge factor in one's level of happiness. Bad relationships result in negative consequences in all aspects of life. Getting engrossed in your work, no matter what you do, will make you selfish. And while you are busy with your shoulder to the grind wheel, you'll miss out on life.

> *"What's money? A man is a success if he gets up in the morning and goes to bed at night and in between does what he wants to do."*
>
> —Bob Dylan

You might not realize it in your 30s or 40s, by the time you are 50, you will start to feel the need of joyful relationships. People you can relate to and will always be there for you. Do not procrastinate on this desire, because the best relationships are built in time and they require attention, dedication and, last but not least, affection.

A general illusion today is one of supremacy: most feel there is enough time to do everything, even if they don't have time (or make time) for everything. The sentiment is: "why do today what you can put off until tomorrow." However, "tomorrow" keeps moving back a day.

No one ever said on their deathbed: "I wish I had worked more and enjoyed life less."

Of those who have received acclaim for their accomplishments, most have not begun with the purpose of making money. Money will not take you there. Passion, dedication and authenticity will.

Just Say No

Ever find yourself in a reactive state? You know, where your routine suddenly slips out of control? Chances are, you say "yes", when you should be saying "no".

Protect your routine by learning to respect your boundaries, because too often you will be the only one respecting them. There really isn't a reason to give excuses why you can't do something (this just encourages argumentative pressure). Just politely explain "No. My plate is full."

Make materialism irrelevant

From grade school, through adulthood and even into our retirement years, we are given a financial consequence for any endeavor we don't allow to entirely consume us. Everything will be fine; all we have to do is follow a specific plan. If we fail to follow the strategy, everything will crumble and we'll end up jobless. Or even worse, homeless.

> *"Money isn't everything. Not having it is."*
>
> —Kanye West

The truth is that money does matter. Of course it does. It is the representation of resources and it allows us to live comfortable lives. However, when money is the ultimate goal, in the end, all you will have … is well … money. Some work hard for money. They endure hardships because of circumstances in their lives. Yet in spite of all difficulties, they still manage to achieve their dreams.

Sylvester Stallone slept in a train station before selling his script for "Rocky." We all know how that movie did. The film company wanted only to buy the script, but Sly insisted on playing the lead character. As you know, he got it his way.

Tyler Perry wrote his first stage play in 1992. Let's just say the production received a "less than favorable" reception. It broke Perry financially. But he never quit. Over the next several years he rewrote the play several times, eventually hitting success in 1998.

We've all heard about the failures of Abraham Lincoln before he won the highest position in the country.

> *"If you fall down 100 times, get up 101."*
>
> —Japanese proverb

Perceive success as something that will open a lot of doors, which will help you learn a lot, but not as something to bring you money. Use and consume material things as much as needed, but never overindulge. We are more than matter. We have a spirit and it needs to be fed.

Learn how you learn

Many people recognize that each person prefers different learning styles and techniques. Learning styles group common ways that people learn. Everyone has a mix of learning styles. Some people may find that they have a dominant style of learning, with far less use of the other styles: Decide which type of learner you are:

- Visual

    You prefer using pictures, images, and spatial understanding. You can easily digest information from things like graphics, videos, cartoons, diagrams, webinars or infographics.

- Aural

    You prefer using sound and music. You'll pick an MP3 file or a podcast over a webinar or article any day!

- Kinesthetic

    You prefer using your body, hands and sense of touch. You need to learn "hands on" – by doing things; jumping right into a new platform or software.

- Verbal

    You prefer using words, both in speech and writing – transcripts, written instructions, articles – in fact, you can read an article faster than you can watch a video.

Once you have determined your best learning style (or styles), embrace it. Toss out that written "To do" list if verbal learning is not your thing. Dictate that article, if you know you're an aural learner. Draw little icon-pictures instead of writing things down or use a mind-map, if you're a visual learner.

If you employ your preferred learning style(s) you'll notice tasks flowing easier and your memory improving, leaving you with more time, focus and energy. You can never have enough of those.

Make the time to make time

Once you educate yourself, you'll notice a change in your habits; you'll spend less and less time with trivial things, freeing up time to focus on what's most important. Become aware of the time factor and you'll put more thought into finding ways to organize your activities efficiently.

Only when you discover what success actually means to you, will you be ready to offer affection and dedication to those around you and concentrate on what makes you happy. You may face some challenges along the way to organizing your time, but that's just because there's so much to do!

Create some daily success habits. Often we overlook the importance of daily habits in managing our lives and ourselves. It's the small changes we make to our daily routines that enable big changes in our lives and careers.

The following exercise will help you build a simple personal framework around which the rest of the day's activities fall into place.

Create an infrastructure so that no matter what happens – you feel calm and assured.

Exercise One

My Top 3 PRIORITIES in life right now are:

1. _____ 2. _____ 3. _____

My Top 3 STRESSORS in life right now are:

1. _____ 2. _____ 3. _____

Exercise Two

What supportive daily habits – SPECIFIC DAILY ACTIONS – could you introduce?

Write up to 5 actions that best support you – including your HOME, PERSONAL and WORK-LIFE. They must be SPECIFIC and MEASURABLE so you know exactly what to do, and can clearly say you have completed the step!

TIP: You know yourself. Where do you sabotage yourself regularly? What ideas do you already (perhaps secretly) have?

Examples:

- Have 15 minutes of silence or alone time each day
- Take 10 mins mid-afternoon to recap where I am
- Eat lunch away from my desk
- Be in bed by 11pm
- Do at least 30 mins of exercise/activity every day
- Connect daily with partner/spouse (5 mins listening)

	Habit	Benefit to me
1.		
2.		
3.		
4.		
5.		

Breaks? Yes please!

If lunchtime is your only break (if you even take that) it won't do. The body and mind need breaks. Olympic athletes discovered this years ago. A former Soviet Union coach name Tudor Bompa discovered a technique he termed "periodization." Basically, he said one should plan periods of work followed by periods of recovery. This was done for both physical as well as mental reasons.

Spending your days sitting at a computer requires a break every hour (two at the max) and use a timer with an alarm to remind you, until it becomes a habit. When the alarm sounds, get up. Walk around. Walk round the block. Do some exercises. Or just lie flat with your legs on a pillow, letting your mind wander and your back rest.

Keep the breaks short—ten to fifteen minutes, max.

Here's why they work: Without the break, maybe you would have went off on a tangent. Maybe you would have gotten super involved in extraneous research. But with the break, you return focused, so things like these are nipped in the bud, so to speak. Now refreshed, you can come up with the perfect opening for your next video. Solutions suddenly present themselves, your day gets back into focus so you can zoom in on your priorities.

Not convinced?

Try this: Track and assess how much you actually accomplish during your regular week. Figure out some way to measure your productivity. Then record it at the end of the week.

The following week add the breaks, track and assess. Was there a difference? Did you get more accomplished, even though you took breaks? The same? Less?

And the reward goes to ...

Fact: When there's a reward at the end of a difficult road, people are far more likely to stay the course. What is your ideal reward for being productive?

Remember, rewards are not always tangible. Sure it's great to eat a truffle every time you exceed seeing three clients a day. But you can also think simple. Like using a Fitbit and give yourself a bounty if you exceed a certain the number of steps; or going for a swim, if you shave an hour off your work time. Wash away the stress of the week in the pool.

The important thing is to identify the type of reward that would appeal to you—and set it up so you can achieve it. If you are allergic to chocolate, a Hershey's Kiss is probably not a good idea for a reward. For the best emotional impact, your prize shouldn't be too difficult to reach, but it also shouldn't be too easy. Eventually you will "train" yourself these routines to become habits.

Make your habits routine and your routines a habit

Success and overall life satisfaction do not come suddenly. You don't accidentally achieve a fulfilling life. You want a full plate of success and satisfaction, be prepared to pay a bill of work and perseverance. Nothing great was ever achieved overnight. You know what they say about the building of Rome. Successful people create routines. Waking up early, meditating, and exercising are some practices that get you ready for the duties of the day and make energy flow.

These are just some pieces of advice about creating "success" from both personal experience and stories of others. The most important fact is this: there is no recipe to success. It means different things to different people. You have to know yourself and do things for your heart before you find your definition of "success."

Chapter Notes

CHAPTER THREE

Balancing Your Home Business and Family Life

Once upon a time, ones business life was confined to a distant and tawdry office building. Thoughts and concerns about work melted away at the (usually male) utterance of, "Honey, I'm home!" Small businesses in home-based offices, with very few, if any employees, were unheard of. But now, new models of how we handle work and fun, family and productivity are evolving faster than the next iPhone update.

In the age of home businesses, anyone from the harried mom of three to the ambitious doctoral student can pursue a multitude of career possibilities. These businesses let you structure your work life the way you want, so missing out on dinner with the family is as rare as Halley's comet. No more answering to the boss who's constantly leaning over your shoulder and looking at his watch as you leave at 4:59. The new way makes working around other commitments easier, but has a huge, potentially dangerous pitfall. It lacks a physical separation between business and pleasure. Before you know it, you have unexpected guests knocking at your door during business hours and the looming deadlines that suck the life out of your spirit.

People think of a home office as a place where they do their work. Don't make this mistake. Housing your workspace is just one of your home office's functions. Instead, think of your office as a tool for running a successful business. It is to your service-based business what a sewing machine is to a seamstress, or a forge is to a blacksmith. If your sewing machine is deader than a doornail or you can't find the lighter to light your forge fire with (an unlit forge is pretty useless), no work gets done.

Here's how you'll spend your working hours:

- The Seamstress with sewing machine problems: You abandon the manufacturer's manual because half way through it, you realize it is incomplete. So you then enter a time sucking void on YouTube looking up videos trying to give yourself a crash course on sewing machine repair. When you finally figure out what you need to do you discover you don't have a screwdriver small enough to remove the foot-plate.
- The blacksmith with an unlit forge: —You spend half a day looking high and low in your blacksmith shop searching for your lighter. You finally come across it and find out that it is empty. Then you jump in your truck and spend an hour and a half running into town, to buy another one.

These sorts of things are what happens to your productivity when your home office is disorganized. You lose productivity, energy—and, oh yea, hours of time.

Disorganization is:

- Tiring
- Frustrating
- Stress-producing
- Energy consuming

- Time-eating
- Depressing

You could say disorganization is contagious. (You know how it is, you let one tiny, disorganized area go for a little bit and it snowballs into an avalanche.)

Organize your home office to maximize productivity in your business – soon you'll be getting stuff done!

Make a Plan, Stan

(Even if your name isn't Stan, this section still works.) Whether your office is just a wee bit cluttered, with one or two "trouble spots"… or buried under a mountain of chaos and dust-bunnies, organizing it will maximize your productivity. Even the payoffs from a 10% boost in productivity are impressive.

Sure, cleaning is great, especially if the cleaning yields a couple of those big black industrial garbage bags of dirt and junk. But that's only one step. You also need to do some serious analysis, planning and decision-making.

Clutter and imbalance is not always a symptom of sloppiness or procrastination. It's not even a sign that a tribe of sixteen year olds have been thundering around the house, destroying everything in their path (even if this is actually going on at home). More often than not, it's a clear sign that something is not working.

We can deal with this. Are you ready?

Essential Steps to Get Started

1. Develop checklists
2. Beautify your workspace
3. Schedule time
4. Ask for help
5. Don't lose yourself

Let's look at each of these steps individually:

1. Put "make checklists" on your checklist

Every business has projects and tasks that are constantly repeated. Such as:

- Write a blog post every week.
- Send an email to your list every day.
- Create a new product each month.
- Make sales calls every day.

Whatever it is, if you're doing it more than once, it's checklist worthy.

Checklists ensure:

- That the task is done correctly. For example; if you have a history of sending bad links to your email list, a checklist with an entry that says: "send a test email and check links" will help put an end to this embarrassing faux pas. We all know of a story where someone sent an email meant for a spouse or lover to a business contact by accident. Oops.
- Projects are completed quickly. There are few things less productive than re-inventing the wheel with each new product launch (counting

the pages of paper in a ream of copy paper to make sure you get the full 500 is slightly less productive. Maybe.) Create a checklist, and you'll always know exactly what needs to be done, and when.

- Hand off tasks you don't like. Having your systems documented with checklists makes it super easy to hire a virtual assistant to help manage those mundane, un-fun tasks you're doing. Unless you enjoy the mundane and un-fun.

2. Pretty up your workspace

While it might seem tempting to misconstrue work-from-home as work-from-bed, having a separate workspace is essential to your business. Whether it's a separate room, or a desk with everything within reach, it's important to have a designated work area. It's just short of flashing red sign that says: "I'm working, and cannot be disturbed." It also lays the foundation for a good work ethic. A good work ethic never got anyone into trouble.

Make sure it's organized and make sure it's clean. It doesn't have to be operating room sterile, but you don't want to have to wear a respirator mask to step inside. While at first, it might seem like you have some sort of a system "in your head", it rarely stays that way. When your work space is organized and free of clutter, funny enough, so is your mind. Not too long ago, there was a popular expression "a cluttered desk is a sign of a cluttered mind." That expression gave rise to an entire industry designed to help business executives clean their desktops as a sign of their mental keenness. Everything feels more streamlined and less overwhelming. It never, ever hurts to be over-organized.

Let's not forget to have fun with it! Whether it's a tiny dustbin for shredded paper, a collage of people who inspire you, inspirational quotes written on the wall or a jar of happy thoughts, customize your space to inspire you and anyone who steps in. It's an office space, not a jail cell.

Exercise One

1. Set an hour aside every week to de-clutter. This includes the files in your cabinet, the papers on your desk and even organizing folders in your laptop. While this might sound like a thankless task, it can be a real stress buster. And this hour can easily save two or more hours later in the week by increasing productivity.

Declutter Your Home Office Checklist

- ☐ Dedicate a drawer to files and assign folders.
- ☐ Sort papers. Shred sensitive information. Papers left go in folders.
- ☐ Remove items from the office that don't belong there.
- ☐ Clean out desk drawers and restock any needed supplies.
- ☐ Discard empty or unusable pencils, pens, markers and other items.
- ☐ Dust all surfaces. Wipe down if possible or necessary.
- ☐ Clean computer monitor and spray keyboard with compressed air to clean.
- ☐ Organize bills, mail, home binder etc.

2. Make an oasis. Ok, so now you've taken care of the essentials. Time to make sure that your home office serves one other, vital function – that it provides you with maximum:

- Inspiration
- Creativity
- Energy

Make sure it becomes a stress-free sanctuary where you pursue your life's passion. This could be a simple placement of candles, plants, flowers, pictures, sculptures/figurines, or a water feature. Don't skimp on these accessories. If it makes you smile or helps your relive stress, it's worth finding and place for.

I Will Make Space for the Following in my New Office

- ☐ _____
- ☐ _____
- ☐ _____
- ☐ _____
- ☐ _____
- ☐ _____
- ☐ _____

3. Flex your schedule. Experiment with the hours you'd frequent your workspace. Since you're your own boss, you needn't stick to the 9-5 schedule. You could devise hours that really work for you, and break times that work for you and your family. Kick that punch clock to the curb!

Remember why you're doing this

Did you always want to be a content editor? Does working with children fill you with a thrill of fulfillment? Write this motivation down. Look at it several times. There will be days when you'll find it easy to forget why you're doing what you do. When a family emergency shortens your work deadline, or you take on more than you can chew, you might find yourself starting to view your work in terms of "finishing" and "getting it over with". During these times, take a peek at your motivation statement. Remember why you picked your profession.

Take deep breaths, go for a walk and ask yourself to slow down. Summon the energy that filled you before, the reason why you liked doing it in the first place. Have those ultimate, wholesome goals impose their will over your anxiety, fears, and stress. You'll be okay (and remember to take it easy next time).

Exercise Two

1. Set up a whiteboard. Pin your best work moments on it. Be as specific as possible: feedback from a client that made you smile, a piece that surpassed your expectations or insights you gained. If it doesn't put a smile on your face, it doesn't go on the board. When you're verging on a burnout, you now know where to look.

2. Space out your work tasks. Only take on as much as you can handle. Sure, you may end up meeting that impossible deadline once, but is it worth the stress and toll it took on you? The wrinkle or the grey hairs it gave you won't go away. Does this additional task further your vision, or leave you with such breadth of responsibilities that you can never go into the depth that each one deserves?

3. Put fun on your schedule

I'll give you a life-changing tip. Instead of scheduling your work commitments first, start with planning your holiday and family fun. Plan your holidays, really giving them some thought. This will give both you and your loved ones something to look forward to all year.

Now you wait for your calendar to clear up before you take your son and daughter to the Wizarding World of Harry Potter. And more often than not, you decide you just can't make the time for it. Years from now your kids are adults telling a therapist how they have trust issues from you lying to them and saying this is the year we go to Harry Potter World. Avoid this trauma for your family, book your tickets at the beginning of the year. It won't hurt, I promise. Make sure you can turn "off" your work appointments during this time (yes, your smart phone too), so that both you and your family get the quality time you guys deserve. I know what you are thinking: "But with my work, I can't do that." To which I say "yes you can."

Exercise Three

1. Buy a calendar and hang it up in your office. Mark your work deadlines in red AFTER you've finalized your family dates in green. Make sure there's enough of both every month!

2. Make sure your family appointments are set in stone just like your work appointments. Make moving family engagements as difficult as it is to move work engagements. Book your vacations, and make a non-refundable deposit. This way, you won't end up cancelling or shifting around your personal dates for work, unless it's extremely important.

4. You can ask for help. Really.

You know those weeks when you're strapped to your work chair, and house chores make you feel like a sloth on Xanax? Or the weekends you spend with family and that results with you blowing off work deadlines? It feels like you need to do it all or give up everything, that's really not the case.

You've got some drama. OK, you have a lot of drama. And, you're so caught up in it; you forget that you can ask for help. Or you refuse to admit you need some help. Delegation is an art and a godsend during these oh so desperate times (I'm putting the back of my hand against my forehead for effect here.) It's actually not all that dramatic. Try to spend more time on the parts of home and work that you enjoy. Devote less time on obligations you hate, to create a more optimal balance.

When the going gets tough, it's important to have a support system in place. Having a home business can feel isolating at times. Your phone and computer become your sole connections to the outside world. You're not part of a bustling office where you automatically make connections or have conversations by the water cooler. If you can open up to at least one or two people at home or in connection to work, you've got half the equation right.

Exercise Four

1. Outsource tasks. Especially the ones you'd rather not personally take on. Cleaning the house? Hire a maid. Administrative work tasks? Try a virtual assistant. Hiring help does wonderful things for your schedule! Take a minute and create your list now. What will you outsource?

Outsource List

- ☐ _____
- ☐ _____
- ☐ _____
- ☐ _____
- ☐ _____
- ☐ _____

2. Surround yourself with positive people. Create a circle of people you love and trust, both at work and at home. Talk to them when you're feeling low or overwhelmed. It doesn't make you weak, not at all. What it does do is give you a much-needed fresh perspective.

3. Acknowledge the support of people. You know, the ones who are rooting for you. A simple thank you is all it takes. Make a list of five things you're grateful for. At least once a week pick something from the list and let someone know how much they mean to you.

Tell yourself: "I'm thinking of you."

Blending your work and family life is challenging, it's about as easy as catching a greased pig. And when you leave yourself behind, life can lose all meaning. I've had weeks when I'm so caught up in making time for people and appointments I become a robot. I go to sleep at night without having time to think and reflect on my day. Balancing your work and home business works only when you have a healthy and happy frame of mind. And for that you need to make time for you.

It isn't as easy as just pampering yourself. A weeks' worth of stress and mayhem isn't cured with a massage. Sure, it feels great at the moment. You need to take care of your health every day. Make sure you're hydrated at all times, get enough sleep and keep a fruit basket at your desk to keep snacks on the healthy side. Take short walks when you feel too cooped up, and listen to music to unwind. And oh yea, make the effort to change your playlist from time to time; it gets you out of the rut.

It doesn't mean you can forget about the occasional self-pampering sessions. Take a day off every couple of weeks to catch up with your hobbies and keep up your spa appointment (my personal favorite is my monthly manicure and pedicure). Have a personal project you're working towards, whether it's rereading *Pride and Prejudice* or sampling every Subway™ sandwich. It might seem silly and fun, but it creates a real breather.

Exercise Five

1. Spend at least 20 minutes a day with yourself; unwinding and relaxing.
2. Take a day off each month, just because.

Most importantly, have fun with it. You've started something from scratch on your own! If that doesn't reflect positively on you, nothing does. Be proud of yourself, and enjoy the opportunity to do what you love, with the people you love around you. Go ahead, Tiger, pat yourself on the back.

Working from home is a dream for many. For some it's a nightmare. A distraction-filled, inefficient and disorganized environment that makes work scarier than a monster under your bed. Dread heading into your office every day? Feel you're not as productive as you could be? Guess what, it's time to re-think and re-organize your space.

In the end, it's totally up to you to decide what constitutes a well-functioning, enjoyable home office. You work hard and you've earned that right. If nothing else, don't procrastinate (please, I'm begging you)—take steps to start organizing your home office for minimal stress, maximum productivity and maximum profits today!

Chapter Notes

CHAPTER FOUR

Comfortably Confident

Lemon water cleanses, Pilates, spinning classes, P90X, yoga, calorie counts, green tea detoxes, and eating nothing but cardboard. Just a few of the health trends that have appeared in the last twenty years. OK, maybe not the eating cardboard one. But you know what I am talking about. Aren't these health trends appealing? Good news, you don't have to drink green tea for a month or attend a spinning class six days a week to get the confidence boost you need. I promise.

These health crazes skyrocketed to popularity, it seemed like everyone is or was doing them. When someone loses 15 pounds, is working out every day, eating less, or drinking way too much green tea, people take notice. I understand these health vogues because people think it makes them feel better about themselves. Exercise, in general, is known to be a natural confidence booster, it isn't, however, the only confidence booster.

I give you the authority to be confident

In 2015, William Lee Adams, a London based journalist, published an article about confidence in the *New Scientist* magazine. Adams wrote that in certain situations, "Confidence can affect performance no matter how skilled the person is to begin with." Meaning someone who is considered an expert can still royally botch-up a speech due to lack of confidence. So the question, my dear friends, is how do people get to a point of feeling comfortable in a situation that demands confidence? Perhaps more confidence than you can normally muster. The answer is, (drum roll please) learning how to be authoritative and, you guessed it, feeling comfortable while doing it.

Now imagine someone you consider confident.

- Do they possess an authoritative demeanor?
- Do they seem to take command of the room without visible effort?

Your answer is probably yes. Why? Because authority and confidence go hand in hand. You know, like peanut butter and jelly.

The fight of the century: Confidence vs. Arrogance

During your quest for self-assurance, keep in mind that a very fine line separates confidence from arrogance. Be careful not to cross it. For me, arrogance is when one not only believes they are better than other people (blunder number 1), but also *act* like they are better than other people. (Blunder number 2). Likewise, when one assumes their ideas are better (blunder number 1 again) and then discards feedback and contributions from other members of the team (yup, blunder number 2 again).

On the other hand, a confident person, generally speaking, does not give up and will not give up. You never see them "lose it" because something doesn't work out the way they planned or intended it. There is no freaking out because they believe they are not capable of performing or accomplishing a task or goal. Simply put, a confident person believes that they are capable of accomplishing anything. Their confidence factor does not allow them to be held back by fear. HOWEVER, they don't feel the need to let everyone around them know they are capable of accomplishing anything every 5 minutes. There's a four letter word for those people, starts with the letter J and ends with the letter K. This is not the person you want to be.

Adams also states in his report that certain words, actions, sights, or anything that stimulates nerves can affect how people act without people consciously realizing it. He gives an example of public speakers who stand with "confident poses produce more testosterone which boosts motivation and risk-taking, whereas those that take insecure poses produce more of the stress hormone cortisol." Confident pose? I can imagine the look of confusion on your face. It's what's also known as a high-power pose. An example high-power pose is one foot resting on the other knee, with your hands clasped behind your head. A low-power pose is arms folded in front of you as you slump forward. You get the idea. High-power pose is the confident person who isn't afraid of the guy or girl sitting across the table from them. The confident person is ready to take on the world. The low-power-pose is the one screaming "I might pee my pants any moment now … I'm so sorry."

What other people say (and do) can also affect the subconscious brain. By doing things like holding a powerful stance or taking on the persona of a confident person, you can consciously counteract the negative subconscious processes. If you make yourself aware of the subconscious, you can alter it. When your mother told you to stand or sit up straight, she (possibly unknowingly), helped you create positive, confidence-increasing habits. Nice job, Mom. However, not all thoughts or events affect your brain completely subconsciously.

"High Power" body language (top row)
vs.
"Low Power" body language (bottom row)
(Images courtesy of Amy Cuddy, Harvard University)

A study in the *Academy of Marketing Studies Journal* in 2014 by the authors Greenacre, Ngo Manh, and Chapman stated that one aspect that can "lower self-confidence arises from its relationship with one's sense of control over one's life." Thinking positive thoughts about both the life you lead and yourself are important to gaining the confidence you need. This leads to a comfortable feeling about being authoritative.

Give your authority a great big hug

The definition of authority according to Merriam Webster: "the power or right to give orders, make decisions, and enforce obedience." Meaning the person in charge. It is further defined as: "the confident quality of someone who knows a lot about something or who is respected or obeyed by other people." Meaning they are an expert at something. Confident people naturally have authority because when a person is confident it typically signals that they know a lot about the subject. This inherently gives them authority. Being confident in the privacy of home is significantly different from being confident in front of other people. Making the transition from the former to the latter can be a difficult task. When it comes to embracing the authority, by maybe leading a class, a discussion, or speaking publicly, the relationship between confidence and authority can spin 180° because embracing authority is often intimidating. When people lead a class, discussion, or speak publicly it is because they are comfortably embracing the natural authority they have.

You are asking: "April, how do you embrace your natural authority?" Here's a tip: First, think about why you have authority and why you should feel confident about a particular subject, when asked to elaborate or present on the subject or, when asked to perform a specific task. Here are some thought starters:

- Are you only secure when practicing alone?
- Are you a naturally gifted speaker?
- Have you been familiar with the subject/topic for years?
- Do you have a college degree that relates?
- Have you received formal training that relates?
- Is this your passion?
- Do you have a business that relates?

Dear Self

You have confidence and authority, and when in doubt, dig until you find it. Not with a shovel, it's only a metaphor. This step is simply reassuring yourself of your abilities, without allowing your ego to get so big that your hats no longer fit. You are awesome and are where you are today because you worked hard and with a purpose. It's like the SNL character Stuart Smalley used to say: "I'm good enough, I'm smart enough, and doggone it, people like me."

One method to come to terms with your authority is to write yourself a letter explaining all you have done and what you had to do to get yourself to where you are today.

For some, it may be hard to write a letter boasting about your accomplishments. No one wants to be a braggart. You know, the person everyone hates standing next to at a party. But in order to feel comfortable in your own skin, you have to be proud of yourself, of what you have done. No amount of praise from other people will ever fill the void. Only self-confidence can do that. You first need to find self-confidence while in the comfort of your own home. Then you can take to the stage and show it to everyone else.

I'm going to challenge you right now. Sit down and write yourself a letter, make a list, draw a timeline, or even update your resume. List all of your accomplishments or what you feel makes you qualified for the task. You'll see that doubting your abilities was pretty silly.

Exercise One

1. Choose a date several months (or even years) from today. A date that means something to you – an anniversary or a birthday.
2. Imagine that life has gone rather well. Things have turned out the way you wanted them to. Write yourself a letter telling yourself about the developments in your life. Jot down how your life would feel if you were successful and fulfilled.

   *** A copy of the letter I wrote to myself is at the end of the chapter ***

The Rehearsal

The next step, and possibly the most important one, in feeling comfortably confident is rehearsing being confident. Rehearsing a confident attitude works wonders for your self-assurance. Motivational and public speakers rehearse their speeches repeatedly.

> *"Practice does not make perfect.*
> *Only perfect practice makes perfect."*
>
> —Vince Lombardi

Your favorite talk show hosts have scheduled rehearsals before going on air. Rehearsing can help you become confident in your abilities just like writing a letter would. After you practice your speech, lesson plan, or conversation you may be planning with your boss, you will realize that you are an authority on the subject. You know what? You can conquer the world. You go girl! (Unless you're not a girl, then you go guy!) Listed below are a few things to help you rehearse and feel more confident about yourself. They help you embrace your new authoritative attitude.

- Rehearse in front of a mirror.
  Knowing what you look and sound like helps you become more confident when you are giving a speech or even just carrying on a conversation at a convention. Make up a conversation that could actually take place, then come up with responses for questions people may ask. Say them aloud. I know, I know, it seems silly, but it works. Practicing a speech in the mirror is always a good idea because you can pace yourself, remind yourself to make eye contact with the crowd, and figure out the perfect timing for when you need to smile, laugh, or look down at the podium. (Recording yourself is another great option.)

- Go over what you know. Then go over it again.
  This is particularly important if you are giving a speech, leading a discussion, teaching a class, trying to impress someone, or even attending a class. You do not want to get in front of a group of peers and forget why you are capable. If you go over what you know

several times before the event or meeting, you will be more likely to remember the information and speak confidently. It's no fun getting tongue-tied.

- **When you are rehearsing, minimize thoughts about your weaknesses**
  Of course, you want to give them attention, but do not try to perfect your weaknesses. Instead, look at your strengths. Make them the center of attention. For example, if you own a bakery and your chocolate chip cookie recipe is the best thing you make, don't try to make the best cannoli in town. The Italian baker down the street has got those covered. Focus on making the best damned chocolate chip cookies in town.

Exercise Two

1. Think of a time that you felt really confident. We all feel confident at one time or another. Yes, I mean you. You may be confident at work, you may be confident with your friends or maybe you're confident at a daily task like making your family breakfast. What are you confident at doing? Imagine you were confident right now, how does that feel to you?

2. As you remember feeling confident, you will start to feel confident. Think about this confident feeling you are now honed in on. Where in your body does this feeling of confidence start from? Your stomach? Your feet? Your head? Think about your feeling of confidence – where does the feeling start in your body?

3. Imagine you could see this confident feeling. What color is it? Now make this feeling brighter and stronger.

4. Does your confident feeling, feel hot or cold? Either way, double the temperature of your confident feeling.

5. In what direction does your feeling spin? When you feel confident the feeling will spin in one direction or another. In what direction does your spinning confident feeling spin? Spin it faster and faster. Don't get dizzy.

6. How much more confident do you feel now? Yea, I know.

Overall, if you remember that confidence comes after you learn to be comfortably authoritative, remember to write down all the reasons why you are qualified, and rehearse everything. I mean everything! You can be the comfortably confident person you want to be. Above all else, remember that physical appearance or doing what is hot matters much less than mental and emotional confidence.

Letter from Exercise One

Dear April,

I just turned 50 and life is damn good! I'm sitting at my desk, in my office, looking out at my staff and can't believe I am here. My business has flourished. I have several clients on retainer, with a waiting list of a few more. I love being able to assist clients in developing their dreams, finding The Life You Crave. My work is interesting and challenging and I get to choose my hours. My son not only has his undergraduate degree, he has almost completed his graduate degree. My husband and I are planning our annual anniversary vacation and this year we're finally taking a three-week island/cruise combo trip. My relationship with my husband continues to flourish. We both continue to enjoy spending quality time together. I'm feeling fit and continue to exercise regularly.

Chapter Notes

CHAPTER FIVE

Overcoming Setbacks

Maggie found a lump in her breast. Her doctors told her it was malignant. Maggie was distraught, but not defeated. With the support of her family and friends, Maggie had a lumpectomy, in short, a removal of the lump. She has since been through several cycles of chemotherapy and radiation treatments. Maggie has now been cancer free for five years.

Ken had been married for thirty years. The marriage had grown stagnant now that the children were gone and he longed to renew the excitement he and his wife Margaret once had. Unfortunately, they failed to do that. So, Ken found that excitement with someone else. Even worse, Margaret caught him in the act. They both decided they didn't wish to throw away thirty years together, they went to counseling and will celebrate their 35th wedding anniversary next month.

Paula had many years of dedicated service to her company. She was called into her manager's office eager to receive news of a promotion. Instead Paula was thrown for a major loop. She was told that her services would no longer be needed after the end of the week. Paula was determined not to let herself be conquered. Today, she is the owner of a popular and extremely profitable hair salon – which was a lifelong dream of hers.

These are actual people and actual events, not examples I made up to make a point. Take a moment right now and think –do you know people with similar setbacks? How many setbacks have you yourself encountered? One thing I can 100% guarantee you is that we've all had setbacks at one point or another in our lives. What's important, however, is how you responded to these setbacks. Were they used as a catalyst, making the appropriate adjustments to getting your life back on track or did you allow them to consume and control your very existence? I've created some food for thought outlined in this chapter. Little tidbits for you to consider the next time life deals you a setback.

Acceptance is therapeutic. Denial, umm not so much

How did you handle the last crises that either happened to you or had a direct impact on your life? Did you brush it off and get right back in the saddle again? Or, did you wave the white flag and retreat to your bedroom for the weekend (or for the month)? The first step to conquering any setback, hurt or failure is to accept it. I give you permission to do just that. Luckily, I have been ordained as "the person who gives permission to accept setbacks." I allow you to acknowledge the situation or the problem. Because only then can you move forward and allow your resiliency to spring into action. Only when Ken finally confessed his dissatisfaction with his marriage to Margaret, were they able to work on the problem together. It was a difficult task to work to find a common solution that they both could commit to, but ultimately it saved their marriage.

Want to *never* get past a setback? Here's how: convince yourself that your current situation cannot be overcome. Or better yet, tell yourself that whatever is holding you back from moving past your setback is beyond your control. In case you missed it, that was sarcasm. On a serious note, do not give away your power. In my experience whenever I have faced setbacks head on, I find myself in a better position to influence the next phase of my life. When a setback occurs, take that time to reflect and reset.

Exercise One

Make a list of the most recent setbacks you have faced or are currently facing today. Then recall how you handled (or are handling) them. Make a mark in the appropriate column to show whether you faced it head on or gave your power away by denying it.

	Problem	Accepted	Denied
1.			
2.			
3.			
4.			
5.			

Professional Support

There is a misconception, particularly in the black community, about asking for help. Especially for black women – we seldom ask for help (even when we really need it). We've been told that we're supposed to be "strong," and the strong don't need the help. Unfortunately, many of us associate asking for professional help as a sign of weakness. What a crock of ... (you know what). Readers, I beg you, please enlist the help of support groups or professionals who have expertise in how to get you through your current barrier/setback/challenge. In Maggie's case, her affiliation with the local *Susan G Komen for the Cure Foundation* was exactly what she needed to cope during her treatment.

Dial 800-I-need-help for assistance

Here are some questions that may help you pinpoint the type of help you may need and who to approach when asking for this help:

1. What would a home run in your life look like this month?
2. Finishing what task or project this week, would make you jump for joy?
3. In what area of your life are you facing uncertainty or confusion?
4. Do you know someone who might be able to offer assistance?
5. What expertise do you lack that would help you hit a home run in your life? A Professional Coach? Pastor? Therapist?

Your Very Own Friends and Family Plan

Step one to the Family and Friends plan: Assemble a strong, personal support system (whether family, friends or both) to promote your efforts. Maggie's family was limited. Her mother had died when she was only seven years old; she had no siblings and had lost touch with her father long ago. But once the team was assembled, her friends never left her side throughout her long hospital stay and grueling physical rehabilitation. When friends asked if there was anything they could do, Maggie didn't hesitate to ask for help with meals, transportation and household tasks until she was able to get back on her feet. There was zero reason for Maggie to feel weak for asking. She knew ahead of time, the team she had assembled would never make her feel that way.

Maybe you already have a team in place but you just never happen to think of them in this manner. To qualify for your personal support system, members should be more of a help than a hindrance. Certain people weigh us down more than they lift us up. Your support elevator should only possess an up button.

Here's a quick checklist to determine who should be on your support team and who shouldn't:

- Do those folks you turn to truly support and uplift?
- Are their deeds constructive or discouraging?
- Do you feel better when they're around? Or, do you feel drained?
- If your relationship was IDEAL, what's one thing that would be different?

It's important for you to have the right team to help navigate your setbacks and trials, but it's equally important to be willing to be a member of someone else's support team/system. You will unknowingly gain value that will/can help you with your future setbacks. Plus, its just good Karma.

Impose an Embargo on Negativity

Holding on to negativity (you know what I mean, like that anger you've built up because you were treated unfairly) sucks away our time, energy, and creativity. It should come as no surprise that this prevents you from moving forward fruitfully. Tackling your setback head on requires your ability to squash any negative emotion. You aren't in denial. You're refocusing your attention on getting past your setback.

Exercise Two

Tune out anything that falls outside of your sphere of control and authority. Once you've accomplished that, ask yourself the following questions:

1. What am I afraid of?
2. Why am I afraid?
3. What can I do right now to improve this situation?
4. What is my excuse for not taking action?
5. What is my excuse for not …?

Put a String on your Finger to remember Gratitude

Ok, not literally with the whole string thing, but definitely remember gratitude. Gratitude reminders are a perfect way to remember that although you are dealing with a setback, things could definitely be worse. Go ahead and complete the exercises below. They will help you keep things in perspective by serving to bring more appreciation, gratefulness, and thankfulness into your life.

Start your day off right. In the morning, you pour yourself that wonderful cup of coffee (or tea or juice, etc.) We all love that moment, don't we? Do yourself a huge favor; take this moment to think about all the things that you're thankful for. Everyone has some things to be thankful for. Yes, everybody.

Here are some examples:

- The simple fact that you woke up this morning
- The beautiful morning
- The promise of the day
- The calm before the day officially begins

There are about a zillion things you take for granted that you rarely are grateful for. Don't believe me? Try this: Imagine losing some of these things you take for granted. Like say, your ability to walk, your ability to process information (meaning to think), a friend, your home, your job or anything that currently provides you comfort for that matter. Now imagine getting each one of these things back, one by one. How grateful would you be? Kind of makes a lot of problems seem trivial, doesn't it?

Let's be realistic, things will not always go your way. Don't only depend on gratitude when things are going well. For those pesky times when things aren't going so well, let's keep things in perspective and be gracious then, shall we? Try asking yourself the following questions:

- What can I learn from this?
- How can I benefit from this?
- What's good about this?
- Is there something about this situation that I can be grateful for?

Exercise Three

November is the month that we Americans officially set aside as a time to be thankful. You know, that food fueled holiday known as Thanksgiving. Even the name has the word "thanks" in it. But it's not the only month we should focus on being thankful. Use the following exercise anytime as a reminder of what you have to be thankful/grateful for.

Create a Gratitude Tree. Gather tree branches, a vase, rocks or marbles, string or ribbon, and cutout paper leaves (from a template like the picture below). Now assemble the tree branches in the vase and secure it with rocks or marbles. Using the cut-out leaves, write thankful thoughts with a gel pen. Then attach the leaves to the branches using string or ribbon. A little craft project that is also good for the soul.

Diligence and Commitment

Make sure you possess diligence and commitment throughout your setback and maintain it during your comeback. Most growth and healing comes during setbacks (i.e. times of trouble). Readers, a little advice from someone who has experienced setbacks: keep your eyes on the goal, not on the difficulty at hand.

> *"With great power comes great responsibility."*
>
> —Uncle Ben to Peter Parker (Spiderman)

Approach, preparation, and action. The power is yours and yours only. Only you have the ability to deal with a setback. You can't foresee the future or the ultimate outcome (unless you have a legitimate crystal ball), but you can act in a manner that produces a more positive outcome. Unexpected (and sometimes unconceivable) obstacles constantly litter our road to recovery. By relentlessly seeking to improve your reaction to obstacles and by maintaining your commitment to overcoming them, you can train yourself to establish new habits to act upon. The other option is to allow yourself to be held hostage by external forces beyond your control. Not such a good option.

If you were to speak with Ken, Margaret, Maggie or Paula today, they would agree that these elements are essential to achieve success when combating setbacks. For me personally, it always starts with my willingness to accept my circumstances so I can then move to the next phase in my "happily ever after" life. Once I commit to that decision, help somehow reveals itself. And even though it's not always easy, everything else just falls into place.

Chapter Notes

CHAPTER SIX

Learning Knows No Age Limit

The term "college student" instantly suggests a just post-pubescent kid, right out of high school, trying to find their way in the world by exploring, learning, and growing. Why this image? Because not all college students fit this stereotype. This idea of typecast can discourage older adults looking to further their education. Thankfully more and more adults are realizing, "yes, I can go back to college." In 2009, students aged 25 and older accounted for roughly 40 percent of all college and graduate students, per the National Center for Education Statistics. That figure is expected to rise to 43 percent by 2020 as 9.6 million older students head to campus. Students over age 35, who accounted for 17 percent of all college and graduate students in 2009, are expected to comprise 19 percent of that total by 2020.

Invest in the Best Investment ... Yourself

Although the idea of older adults going back to college is becoming more and more accepted, the transition into the new, fast paced digital world that lecture halls have become can be intimidating. Kids today know how to jail break a smart phone before they graduate middle school. Possibly making you feel left behind. Don't feel that way.

Making the decision to go back to college is a huge one and has the possibility to change your life for the better, but also for the worse. We've all heard the horror stories of graduates being $200,000 in debt and can't land a job. But play the "furthering your education" game smartly; success can be right around the corner.

Is college right for me?

How do I know if college is for me, or if I am just contemplating it because going to college "seems logical"? Before making that decision, ask yourself the follow:

- Can I afford it?
- Am I willing to take out student loans?
- What will I major in?
- What skill(s) do I want to learn?
- Can I make money with this new skill?
- Why do I want to go back to college?
- Will my family be understanding/supportive?

Asking yourself these questions will help you form a more concrete plan for furthering your education. Once you have a solid plan and put the dream of college into realistic terms, there'll be less room for doubt and error. While asking yourself the questions listed above, it may trigger more personal questions you should be asking yourself before making the jump back into the classroom. That's okay, every person and experience is different. College is a serious decision that effects your time, your wallet, and your mental and emotional health – which can amount to increased stress. So, unless you've recently said "Boy, I wish I had some more stress", its not exactly a good thing. College is a decision that requires a bit more consideration than "What flavor ice cream should I get?"

Cast Your Net(work) Deep and Wide

OK, so you've seriously thought about going back to college and decided to take it further than a passing thought, I offer you this … go for it! There are many wonderful opportunities on college campuses; one of the biggest is the ability to network. Good news, there are no associated fees when taking advantage of these resources.

There are all different types of people in college you get to know. Then you get to know the people they know. The next thing you know you have this vast network of many connections. Networking is a real thing that gets you jobs. The old saying "it's not what you know, it's who you know" isn't completely true, but it isn't completely untrue either.

If you aren't on Facebook, Twitter, and Instagram, you will be. College students love social media and their way of staying in touch with each other is by "adding" or "following" and saying it in 140 characters or less.

Another tip for networking mentioned in the *Huffington Post* is being extremely open about your career goals. In other words, don't be afraid to tell people what you want to do. You never know, they might just have an aunt who can help you get a job in the field. Likewise, look for people who are likeminded or have the same major, there's a really good chance you'll be working with them someday. Or even for them.

Not to mention that interacting with interesting people as part of a college cohort has the potential to open your mind to something you did not even know existed.

Age Is Only an Integer

Even with all the amazing opportunities and possibilities in the college classroom/community you may have to constantly battle your insecurities. Being surrounded by people much younger and sometimes brighter tends to do that to you. Just keep reminding yourself, you are never too old to take a college course or make the decision to return to/start college. Think of a mistake you have made at any point in your life and how you learned from that mishap. These kids don't have the experience you do. As my friend used to tell his son: "I've already forgot more than you know."

- Doreetha Daniels, was a 99-year-old woman who graduated from College of the Canyons with an associate's degree. *USA Today* reported in 2015, that she started her college journey in 2009 because she wanted to better herself and even suffered strokes during the process, but still managed to finish. Sadly, many 20-somethings don't possess her drive.

- When she was close to 50 years old, Cyndi Hutchins, now director of financial gerontology at Bank of America Merrill Lynch, returned to school while keeping her full-time job, earning a graduate degree in gerontology from the University of Southern California. After more than 20 years in financial services, she said, "I had an interest in taking my career in a different direction, and one I felt to be a more personally meaningful direction."

- Valora Reid Bishop, was a 30 something wife, mother of two and full-time government worker, when she decided it was time to stop regretting her lifelong desire to be a college graduate. She said "I was nervous, but thrilled with the opportunity." Valora graduated in 2005, earning a degree in Business from Kaplan University.

- While keeping my full-time employ with the Federal Government, April B. Jones, your author, returned to college as a full-time student and divorced mother of a toddler at the age of 28 to complete my undergraduate degree. By age 36, I had obtained a Bachelor of Science from Kaplan College (now University) and a double Master of Science from both Capitol College (now Capitol Technology University) and Syracuse University.

Furthering your education can take place at any point in your life. Contrary to popular belief, you **can** teach an old dog new tricks. Especially when you consider the extensive tutoring and help available to college students. It is never too late to continue your education.

Be Optimistic about Optimism

Occasionally remind yourself to keep an open mind when you return to college. Colleges center on the idea of promoting new and different ways of thinking. Having an open mind will help you fight insecurities that say, "I can't do it" or "I am too old" or "This is too hard."

> *"Education truly is the arm that can be used to change the world."*
>
> —NELSON MANDELA

The only approval needed to further your education is your own. If mentally fighting your insecurities isn't working, try this: put your thoughts on a page and read them out loud. See just how silly some of your worries are? I thought so. Any that still poses a concern after reading aloud can be reconsidered. However, try to think this time in terms of, "how can I get around this" or "how could I make this go away?" If you can find a solution to the rest of the insecurities left on the page, you'll be ready for the adventure that is college.

Exercise One

Consider your pros and cons of continuing your education. List them here:

Pros	Cons

Show Me the Money!

I know what you are thinking: "April, I just can't afford to go back to college." Good news, there are a multitude of ways to help finance your tuition. There are grants, scholarships, company sponsorships and incentives.

The government offers literally thousands of scholarships for qualified individuals. Some are even geared toward returning college students. A Google search can offer up truckloads of information on availability and applying for one (or even a few).

Talk to your employer to find out if your company helps its employees who want to go back to college. You'd be surprised how many companies offer this assistance. *Business Insider* recently listed Apple, AT&T, Bank of America, Boeing, Best Buy, Disney, Home Depot, and UPS as just a few of the companies that assist their employees with tuition reimbursement. How about talking to your family? Many companies offer scholarships to the children and spouses of their employees. A little bit of effort on the front end of your college endeavor can save you tons on the back end.

Ladies and Gentlemen, in the center ring: The Balancing Act

You hear the term "work – life balance" thrown around all the time. You will be juggling work, school, and family. By taking on classes you subsequently will be cutting the time spent in other areas. How willing are you to make that sacrifice? How willing are they? Even if you aren't sure of those answers yet, there are a few things you can do to get your balancing act together.

Exercise Two

Start by creating a calendar. This way you and your family can see just how much you are doing every day. Write your class times, assignments, tests, projects, presentations, and even work projects on the calendar, but also schedule blocks of time for you to spend just with your family. Working your family's events (like soccer games, recitals and date night) into your calendar is a good idea too. This way, everyone has a visual reminder of obligations and activities.

Dedicated Space

I read a great article from The University of Wisconsin, Green Bay. They suggest creating a space in your home that is strictly for course work. This way, when your family sees you in that space, they will know you are working and not to be disturbed. They also suggest trying to integrate your kids into your course work by asking them to "help" in some way.

Maybe they can quiz you with flashcards you've made. Informing your spouse about what you do while at school is another technique. It is important because they will now feel a part of your endeavor.

Keeping yourself sane during this trying period will be important to your studies, family, and self-esteem. Schedule blocks of time for you to take a hot bath, or go for a walk by yourself. It isn't easy, but it doesn't have to be a circus act.

One Size Does Not Fit All

Continuing your education has never been easier with colleges offering online, evening, night, and even weekend classes. You can take on as many or as few classes as you wish, so you can go at your own pace. Some continuing education online programs allow you as much as nine months to finish a class.

Options such as these make it easier to start your path toward earning your college degree. Nonetheless, if you commit to this goal, always remember, this is an investment in yourself. By putting in the time, money, and effort required to earn a degree (not to mention some new skills) you will eventually reap the rewards.

Get ready to get your geek on

During your college experience, you may be tested not only academically but also technologically. Most modern-day professors endeavor to stay current on all the latest classroom technology. Don't expect all your classes to be strictly lecture. More and more classes are moving toward smaller rosters and teaching methods that necessitate more student interaction.

Today, assignments and grades are often posted online rather than in class on paper, but don't let that scare you. More than ever professors are accommodating all types of students and are becoming more willing to help with personal struggles. Many campuses feature a technical support office or help center where your fellow students can help you navigate through technology.

Remember to appreciate every experience you have in college, and to find the good in every situation. I guarantee this will help you reach your goal of earning a degree. Connecting with new people every day is a benefit of the college experience on which you cannot put a price tag. As challenging as a day may be, remind yourself that you made this decision. You are learning something new every day, and you are investing in yourself. Not a bad deal. So, you can see, there is light at the end of the tunnel. Now go to class!

Chapter Notes

---------- CHAPTER SEVEN ----------

Coping and Control: Managing Stress

Three things in life are certain: Death, Taxes and Stress. Stress is unavoidable. So is anxiety and spells of depression. As we all know ,life can throw curve balls at us and then kick us while we're down. Sometimes life is wearing stiletto heels when it kicks us. Unfortunately, there are issues that are just unavoidable, so it's okay to worry, stress-out, and be sad for a period. As long as it's a short period of time.

In the mental health world, anxiety, stress, and depression go hand in hand. Each one affecting the other two. Stress can increase anxiety and the perspective you have of your life (i.e. make you depressed). The Anxiety and Depression Association of America (ADAA) says that when periods of worry, stress, and depression turn into a constant and uncontrollable feeling that interferes with your life, there's a good chance you have either an anxiety disorder or depression. There are many disorders that a doctor or counselor can diagnose.

The Only Thing We Have to Fear is Stress Itself

The ADAA states that 3.1% of Americans suffer from Generalized Anxiety Disorder (GAD), that's almost seven million people. They go on to list the following disorders (number of Americans affected in parentheses):

- Panic Disorder (2.7%)
- Social Anxiety Disorder (6.8%)
- Phobias (8.7%)
- Obsessive Compulsive Disorder – OCD (1.0%)
- Post-Traumatic Stress Disorder – PTSD (3.5%)
- Major Depressive Disorder (6.7%)
- Persistent Depressive Disorder (1.5%)

Women are more likely than men to have GAD, Panic Disorders, Phobias, and PTSD. Figures, another way we get the short end of the stick.

> *"The greatest weapon against stress is our ability to choose one thought over another.*
>
> –William James

Depending on your job environment and stress and anxiety triggers, the stress that occurs naturally in the work place can be detrimental to your physical and mental health. The following are key factors in the contribution of increased stress and anxiety levels:

- Deadlines (taking on too much)
- Interpersonal relationships
- Dealing with multiple or complex issues

- A job that never ends
- Money Issues
- A job you don't like
- Constant caregiving
- Striving to be perfect
- Disorganized clutter

Customer service jobs tend to cause higher stress and anxiety levels. That's because these jobs have an increased number of personal interactions. I'm sorry to say, we aren't always nice to each other. Stress in the workplace is not limited to customer service jobs. Those increased stress levels you acquire at work can follow you home and impact your life and relationships outside the work place. Learning to control your stress and anxiety at work is vitally important because it takes its toll on "non-work you" and your family. You often hear people say "Don't take work home." That doesn't mean not to take home files or paper work. It means don't take your emotional baggage home. However, this is a two-way street because you can also transport the anxiety and stress from home to work, where it can affect performance and relationships with coworkers. Ask yourself the following questions:

1. Where do I add stress to my life?
2. How do I react when I am feeling stressed?
3. Who am I trying to please?

Deadly Triggers and Happy Triggers

Each human body and brain is different. Just like fingerprints. Each brain is configured with its own amount of resilience ... the ability to snap back. Scientists and doctors don't know what part of the brain controls human's resilience, but wherever it is, it deals with a person's ability to bounce back after dealing with tough situations. It also determines how someone handles several stressors or anxiety triggers. We all know people who can carry the weight of the world on their shoulders while maintaining a smile. We also know those who encounter the smallest bump in life and fall apart. I know … I'm rolling my eyes too.

Everyone has his or her own amount of resilience, which also means each of us has our own unique breaking point … the stage where we can't bounce back as quickly or take on one more worry without having a panic attack, a breakdown, or just feeling defeated. Resilience is measured by the amount of time it takes an individual to bounce back to their normal state. Obviously, each person has a different rate. Those with anxiety tend to have lower breaking points and longer bounce back periods. Learning to control stress and anxiety involves figuring out just where that breaking point is. Once that point is discovered, we must learn to take a step back when being pushed near our threshold and "reset" ourselves for the day.

"Resetting" can be difficult to do when at work because it usually requires a little time to escape. There are, however, ways to manage your stress and anxiety levels without having to stop working for long periods of time. Staying productive at work while still managing your stress and anxiety levels is difficult because there tend to be many natural negative triggers or stressors in the work environment. This is exactly why the workweek was revamped to have "weekends", time to recharge for the next work cycle. The negative triggers are made up of things you can't control like:

- A coworker or boss being in a bad mood
- A coworker forgetting to clean the microwave
- A client being unhappy
- Any other event (small or large) that takes a toll on your mental state.

HOW TO DEFINE YOUR DREAMS

Planting positive reminders in your environment can help balance out the natural negatives. Positive triggers can be controlled, and there are many ways to plant them in your life. Here are some examples:

- Putting a sticky note with a sweet message from a loved one in your car for when you are stuck in rush hour traffic (Awwww.)
- A happy note on the inside of your waiter order notepad, (or on a corkboard or another space in your office)
- Tucking a hidden note in the pocket of your purse or wallet

Any place that you see repeatedly every day is a great spot for a positive trigger. Forgetting it's there and finding it again is a sweet surprise.

If having a loved one write sweet notes isn't appealing, (you stone heart you ... just kidding) perhaps doing the same thing for yourself by find planting inspiring quotes, scriptures, lyrics, or any other words that make you happy in spots you will allow you to stumble on them. You can update sticky notes to yourself as often as you like, but having others say encouraging things has more sentimental meaning to it than a Bob Marley quote.

Exercise One

List 5 ways you will inspire your positive triggers:

- Photographs are another great way to reminisce on the happy times in your life. Try changing the background on your phone to someone you love: a pet, a friend, a family member. Apps are available that combine several pictures into one image so you can have multiple photos or even photos with a positive quote on your lock screen. Print and frame photos and place them on your desk, walls in your office, and your locker at work. Set your background image on your computer to a photo you love.

Again, if having photos of your loved ones everywhere isn't your thing, then find some beautiful, artistic photos that you can get lost in. Pick images that take you to another place even if it's just for a few seconds. Loosing yourself for even a few moments can help you "reset."

Why Do Today What You Can Put Off Until Tomorrow?

Focusing on breathing is great exercise that can help relax the body. If you do yoga or meditation, you already know this.

Try this when you feel you are nearing your breaking point: inhale while slowly counting to five, and exhale while again slowly counting to five. Do this several times if needed. Likewise, taking a walk, going to grab a snack or drink, or anything else that can get you away from your desk for a few minutes and remove you from stress are good ideas.

If coworkers are a source of the stress (or just annoyance), then leaving for lunch is a great idea. Eating in your car or anywhere away from your coworkers gives you an opportunity for some alone time and allows you to "reset" for the day. Check lists have proven beneficial for those with stress and anxiety because it puts the day's tasks into perspective and allows you to feel a greater sense of accomplishment when you check off a task. Try to keep those to-do lists short so accomplishing multiple tasks is achievable. Constantly remind yourself that you just need to do what needs to be done today.

If things can wait until tomorrow, let them. You might be surprised to find time at the end of the day to do the things you were putting off until tomorrow. Only with this method, there is no stress to get it done.

Avoid conversations or debates you feel passionate about on the more stressful days. Why add fuel to the fire? Disagreeing with someone is in itself a stressful situation; so, on bad days avoid these incidences at all costs.

Smell Your Way to Relaxation

If allowed, listening to music on the job or bringing your pet to work can help relieve stress as well. Many companies are allowing these types of things because they know the positive effects they have on employees.

A more practical and accepted tactic is the scent of lavender. Medical professionals claim that lavender has been used for centuries to promote relaxation. The word itself means: "to wash". Maybe that's because it can wash away stress, since the scent of lavender helps calm and sooth the mind. An air freshener for your car, office or home can help lower stress and anxiety levels. Lavender-scented hand lotions, teas, and other products are also available. If lavender isn't a scent you enjoy, citrus and coconut scents have also been known to help with stress levels.

Giving yourself a massage on your hands, back of the neck, or temples is another great way to take a break and relieve stress while still sitting at your desk. Some companies hire professional masseuses to perform this task. Lucky you if you work at a place that provides this.

An Ounce of Prevention ...

There are lots of little tips and tricks for managing stress, but taking preventative measures is a much better idea. Eating right, exercising, avoiding alcohol and caffeine (or at least restricting them), and getting a good night's rest are all standard healthy habits that also help ward off stress.

Doing things that help you relax is important. Finding time to do them is more important. Whether it be as little as reading a book for thirty minutes a day, to taking an entire afternoon on the weekend to hit golf balls at the driving range. This helps manage stress at work because it serves as a reward for getting through the workday (or workweek).

Working on personal mental health is just as important to a person's wellbeing as a steady income. Some maintain it's even more important.

I can't argue against that. Viewing the reward, or time alone, as valuable to your attitude helps you desire this beneficial act.

Keep Your Morning Routine Very Routine

I know you probably dread the thought, but a morning routine can be extremely beneficial. Especially if it allows for plenty of extra time in case things don't go as planned. And you know how often that happens. By not having to rush out the door, you can crawl out of bed at your own pace, eat breakfast in peace, or maybe even do a morning yoga exercise.

Yoga is extremely relaxing and a great way to start the day. There are tons of free instructional yoga videos on YouTube. Pick one the fits your style and fitness level.

When it is finally time to get in the car and drive off, make sure to get to your destination with about fifteen minutes to spare. This is just to sit in the car, play a game on your cell phone, and reset again before you walk through the doors. Finding "me time" throughout the day helps lower stress levels, you just must find something that will help you relax during that "me time" to "reset".

Exercise Two

How will you adjust your daily routine?

1.

2.

3.

4.

5.

Use Technology

There are tons of apps for IOS and Android that are geared toward managing stress and anxiety. Healthline.com published the 15 Best Anxiety iPhone and Android Apps of 2015 (*http://www.healthline.com/health/anxiety/top-iphone-android-apps#2*). Here are a few of my favorite:

- Headspace – Headspace is made for people who find it hard to make time for relaxation. In just 10-minute sessions, Headspace teaches the basics of meditation. The app also tracks your progress and lets you keep tabs on your friends' practice. If the initial session provides results, you can sign up for the subscription service and access hundreds of hours of additional guided and unguided meditations. Its meditation made easy.

- Relax & Rest Guided Mediations – While group meetings and discussions are always an option, some people find relaxation more easily on their own. This app lets you relax in the space of your own home or office with three guided meditations. Breath Awareness Guided Meditation (5 minutes), Deep Rested Guided Meditation (13 minutes), and Whole Body Guided Relaxation (24 minutes) are designed specifically to help you relax and sink into a peaceful meditation moment.

- Nature Sounds Relax and Sleep – If you find yourself longing for the sound of the ocean to help you relax, the Nature Sounds Relax and Sleep app is for you. Open this app whenever you're feeling anxious or stressed. You can select locations or sounds like the jungle, ocean, or thunder and slip away into a place of relaxation and comfort. If the sounds make you feel sleepy, even better. Use the app to doze off into a relaxing slumber.

I also suggest downloading an easy game that allows you to zone out and focus on something other than the day ahead. This lets you walk into work with a free mind and at break time allows you to take a breather from thinking.

If gaming isn't appealing, you can always find coloring books for adults in stores and online. Yes, I said coloring books. Coloring has been promoted by doctors and other health professionals for adults because it does amazing things for your brain. It can help distract the brain from stresses and anxieties. Here is a popular one you can use on your smart phone or tablet:

Focusing on something so simple but just involving enough to keep you busy can give you a break from the day. Coloring is like a smart phone game, but it allows you to feel as if you are accomplishing something. Coloring is a great task for those who can't seem to sit still. Coloring books are being taken in to meetings, group discussions, and even lecture halls.

If you feel embarrassed carrying a coloring book because it shouts out: "hey everybody, I color!", then doodling might be your cup of tea. A blank sketch book can be picked up at several stores and is less blatant about your relaxing technique. A sketch book also allow you to draw whatever you want instead of staying inside the lines of a coloring book. Which is perfect if you happen to be more of a right-brained thinker.

Drawing the letters to an inspirational quote or scripture is easier than drawing a detailed landscape, but has the same effect. Pinterest and even Google Images have hundreds of quote art options for you to mimic with Sharpies, colored pencils, or even crayons.

These tips and tricks for dealing with work place stress can come in handy, but the most important thing to remember is this: You are not perfect, you are doing the best you can. There are always opportunities to reset and regroup.

Chapter Notes

CHAPTER EIGHT

Finding Your Truth

We live in a world of telecommuting, fast food, 140 character limits (in case you didn't know that is the limit on tweets) and speed dating, so the question is: "is there time to pause?" The much bigger question is: "do you *want* to pause?"

To pause would mean abandoning the concept that life is a never-ending to-do list. Perish the thought (sarcasm intended).

To pause so abruptly would in no way diminish anxieties. You are so accustomed to the hustle and bustle; you may find that you still envision a phantom to-do list hovering around. And when in that moment, you ask yourself: who are *you*? It might even mean wondering where this gregarious-and-affable work/home personality came from. Is that who you are, or are you trying to swim in the tide of expectations from those around you? If you decide that it is time to take a peek within, and connect with your true self – well my friend, you've made an intelligent choice.

Discover the true you

1. Decide what is you and what is "you"

There was an old song during the British Invasion by "The Who" entitled: "Who are you?" It kept repeating the chorus "Who are you? Who? Who?" Likewise, we must keep asking ourselves the same question. One, because we often forget and two, because over time we change as people.

As a teenager, the Kurt Vonnegut quote "*We are what we pretend to be*" had captured my imagination. It opened my eyes to a self that was not just three-dimensional – but layered. The "you" getting through everyday life is a collection of the beliefs you hold (about marriage, love, and how hard you should work, etc.), labels (bubbly, pretty, superwoman) and identifications (mother, wife, kid, adolescent, friend, grandmother, analyst, researcher). There is consistency associated with this "you". As you wrestle your way past each life stage, there is a continuity of who you are at the core that remains the same, even though you as a person have changed. The more things change; the more things stay the same.

Getting started

1. Draw you. Don't worry, you don't have to be Rembrandt. It can even be random words or phrases. Draw the "you" that feels like you in the truest sense; a person loyal to your truest relationships, experiences, interests and values *you* hold dear. Start out with random scribbles; try using your non-dominant hand. This allows you to draw from instinct, rather than what you feel should be the right answer (or what you feel society tells you should be the right answer). Describe what you have drawn in a few key words.

2. Write yourself a eulogy. You may have heard of this before. Imagine you are at a funeral … your funeral (just pretend, no need to commit Hari Kiri).

Who would be in attendance?

What are people saying about you? (Is it nice? Is it bad? Is it juicy?)

What would you want people to say about you?

Write out a eulogy you hope would be written for you. What have you truly given meaning to the time you spent on earth? How far away are you from this person that's in your make-believe eulogy?

3. Write in the 3rd person. How do you see "you"? Take the point of view of an outsider. Now run through your daily routine, significant encounters and relationships over the past week. Write out what you see, but from another person's point of view.

For example: "Works over 40 hours, meets with boyfriend every evening, eats fast food every alternate day, ran into ex-best friend and felt out of place, fought with fussy roommate".

Now play Sherlock Holmes and deduce. From the above example, you can deduce things like: *"dedicated to work" "loyal girlfriend" "Low tolerance for pickiness."* Deductions about who you are will reveal themselves through this exercise.

2. Step away from yourself

So now take the person from step 3 above (the person who is seen through the pretend 3rd party) and compare that person ("dedicated to work" "loyal girlfriend" "fast food-lover") with the person you are. Are they one and the same, or are there stark differences? Be HONEST here girls, now is not the time to sugar coat.

What are the differences? How did they come about? Some may have arisen in pursuit of something that *is* fundamentally you or maybe in a life that is fast paced, leaving *you* behind. Ponder this over as you would ponder over someone else's life —be objective. You need to take a few steps away from yourself before you contemplate it.

Continuing the journey

1. Fill in the chart below. Put the words describing the truest version of you in the first column, and the 'you' you've observed over the past week in the other column. *Are there many consistencies, or inconsistencies?*
2. Reflect on the observed 'you'. How many of your immediate beliefs, thoughts and experiences define you, and how many of them were adopted simply to survive a situation?

You	"You"

Maybe your "Superwoman" persona started out accidentally; someone commented on your ability to get a project done and at the same time get batches of cupcakes ready in time for your little one's school bake sale. As quickly as Clark Kent transformed into Superman in the phone booth, you became Superwoman.

But do you prefer a year-long habit of multi-tasking or are you fundamentally more relaxed? Fast food was the easiest way to find time to do other things during law school, but now you have more time on your hands to cook the healthier kind of food you (and your figure) actually like.

Maybe you value quiet time with friends and family, and yet your time sheet shows you working more hours than necessary in order to earn the big bucks. Maybe you think you value earning big, but then you have a revelation and realize your satisfaction depends on much more than that.

3. Envision letting go. Slowly, gently, imagine yourself letting go of what is not genuine and what is not helping you. I know, I know ... this can be difficult. Who wants to give up the praise and the looks of awe that go along with being given the moniker of "superwoman"? Even if it is at the cost of the leisure time. This reluctance to let it go is perfectly normal. Not being superwoman does not mean you have to gain the title of "slacker-woman." Outsource or drop two of the six tasks you are juggling, and see what that feels like. You might find yourself saying: "Hey, this feels pretty good!"

3. Volunteer for de-zombification

There is a second half to that quote I mentioned earlier:

> *"We are what we pretend to be,*
> *so we must be careful about what we pretend to be."*
>
> –Kurt Vonnegut

We all have a little bit of a persona or facade. Like Mr. Vonnegut explained; the person whom we are pretending to be. This applies not only to personality, but also to the way we handle tasks.

Next time you find yourself doing something just to "get it over with," or parroting phrases that are not what you think, do this: Stop! Ask yourself: "how would I **really** want the task done?" Even if doing it that way might take a little more time out of your schedule. When you look back on it a month from now, will the extra 5 or 10 minutes have altered your life? If I were a betting woman, I would bet no.

Be honest with yourself and think your personal philosophy on getting through various projects. Then communicate these beliefs when people inquire about them. Notice that you feel more vulnerable when you do this, however as you add to your beliefs or they are attacked/questioned by others – it causes some inner dialogue and you grow as a person. (It's ok to question yourself, but *only* if you don't start answering back aloud!) You'll notice that you become better aware of what your core beliefs and values are; eliminating, adding and revising them with life experience.

Keeping it going

1. Keep a journal. Or engage in meaningful conversations or start a blog. When you are truly engaged with an issue, book or person, write (or talk) about it in an appropriate space. Get to the bottom of why this sparked something in you, and what you want to take away from it.

   This might seem irrelevant or too much work, but it doesn't need to be. You need not write an essay – a few words or even posting a picture that summarizes your thoughts about it will suffice. It can even be a simple note App on your smart phone. I find more clarity and a better ability to transfer the findings to my everyday life when I voice out my beliefs and values. This is especially true when I'm in a murky-gray area about something. Instead of "liking" or "disliking" something, I am forced to explore the "whys".

2. Embrace the person that emerges. What emerges is the "you" that is a thinking being, genuine to your participation in life. Take ownership, and responsibility for everything within your grasp. Does the quality of your work, home life and relationships feel the same now, or have you noticed changes? Are you able to put more of yourself into everything you do, rather than letting life get the best of you? If the answer is yes, give yourself a pat on the back. Oh heck, give yourself two pats.

3. Become (more) quiet. Sure, it's tempting to get lost in the noise – to put yourself on default mode. What a luxury, not having to think or be anything more than what your job contract or society expects of you! But not really. Try this: set aside forty minutes a day to clear your head, and get the clarity needed to live life authentically. A walk or bike ride is a great way to re-charge; physically, mentally and emotionally. As you take that stroll, take time to smell the roses, stare into the blue of the sky. Force yourself to notice the buildings

and the people around you. Appreciate, and savor each experience in those forty minutes.

4. Practice observation. Take a few steps back and see yourself and the things around you as they really are. This prevents you from getting sucked into a vortex of drama, instead it keeps you grounded. People who practice meditation or certain schools of yoga know this as "mindfulness". It means "being in the moment", and not the usual drill we all are guilty of, being in one situation, but our minds are in 50 other places. Instead, focus on where you are and what you are doing at that moment. The only time you can change your behavior is right now. You can't go back and undo that mistake you made yesterday. And you can't leap ahead to make sure you perform well tomorrow. All you can do is change how you're behaving right now.

To change your behavior, you must be in the moment. When you're mindful of the present, you're fully aware of what is happening right here, right now. That's when you're able to perform at your peak.

"Mindfulness: paying attention to the present moment with intention while letting go of judgment as if your life depends on it."

–Dr. Jon Kabat-Zinn

4. Live your truth

Getting to the real you is a lot like peeling back a banana. You peel back "coverings" one at a time.

Get out there, bare yourself, and consciously avoid hiding your true self behind expected, default responses. Be aware of every decision you make, every word you write and everything you say, and consistently ask yourself: "Does it come from an authentic space?" If not, get back in there and change the way you are doing things.

Allow yourself to be vulnerable – as much as your mind fights it, fearing rejection, fight it back. I promise you'll be surprised by how quiet, non-conflicted and peaceful you will feel when you stop hiding. Sure, it's easy to cruise along with what is expected of you, doing just enough to get by. However, the highest joy and satisfaction comes from sticking to the values, relationships, decisions and tasks that define *you* in the truest, deepest sense.

Chapter Notes

CHAPTER NINE

Devise a Plan and Get On With It

You have taken the initial step toward devising your plan while reading this book. You have defined your dreams and what success means to you. Your visions of attending or returning to college and obtaining a degree are no longer an unattainable thought. You have used the exercises in this book as tools for being comfortable in your own skin, balancing your home business and family life, and overcoming barriers. You are now armed with awareness, knowledge and additional tools for life's toolkit. Now is the time to get on with it!

The first step to devising a plan is realizing that your plan might not be as simple as you planned (pun intended). By the way, it will also probably not be on the timeline you hoped for. Whether your goal is something you can complete in a year, five years, or even ten years you need to break it down into an easier series of manageable goals. Think of it as a "to-do" list that once completed, becomes your over-arching mission.

Want to know a secret? Devising a plan and creating big changes in your life and business does not have to involve some boring list of dates, milestones and deadlines. In fact, for many creative people, that's just the kind of thing that puts us on edge. We look at that list of dates and milestones and we're instantly overwhelmed, so we file it away for "later." And unfortunately, "later" often becomes never.

Yet that's just how many of us were taught to think about devising a plan(s). We've all heard the expression "A goal without a deadline is just a dream." But sometimes dreaming is what we really need to see a clear path to our destination.

"Everybody has a plan until they get hit."

–Mike Tyson

Plan the work

Let's focus your energy and attention on achieving specific goals in the next six months. These are goals that will align with your long-term beliefs, skills, goals, values and idea of success, all of which you explored with each exercise previously completed.

Goal	Date Achieved
I wrote my vision statement on:	
I set my six-month goals on:	
My six-month goals will be reach on:	

Exercise One

Create an empowering vision for each area of your life – Career/Business, Finances and Wealth, Friends and Family, Recreation and Entertainment, Health and Fitness, Love Life, and Spiritual Development. If you have completed the previous exercises in the book, you will find this easy to do.

What would you be, do and have in each if:

- You could not fail?
- Money was not an issue?
- You had no fear?

Career/Business

Example: I am recognized as an empowering ICF Certified Professional Coach

Finances and Wealth

Friends and Family

Recreation and Entertainment

Health and Fitness

Love Life

Spiritual Development

Recreation and Entertainment

Now work the plan

Rather than a bland calendar or spreadsheet with dates and impressive sounding goals on them, vision boards give you the creativity to let your dreams grow.

Which is more inspiring to you? This:

1. 06/30/16 – Join a Gym and lose 30 lbs
2. 09/30/16 – Launch "Reflection Friday"
3. 10/31/16 – Re-brand "The Business of You"
4. 12/31/16 – Plan romantic escape (Vacation)
5. 12/31/16 – Write and publish first book (The Life You Crave)
6. 5/31/17 – Get PCC ICF Certification
7. 12/31/17 – Write and publish second book (Your Beautiful Business Companion)

Or this:

You see, most goal-setting programs focus on the intended outcome. What is the result you want? And while that's perfect for a business plan, it's really not the best way to keep you inspired and motivated day in and day out.

For that you need to know how achieving your goals will make you *feel*. And that's the real power of a vision board. Your responses from the previous exercise can be used to create a collection of images, quotes and symbols that have meaning to you and which bring out feelings of joy, peace, love and happiness. *They* represent your plan.

Exercise Two

Create your vision board – a "board" that encapsulates your "plan." Take out old magazines and newspapers, and follow your instinct in cutting out pictures and quotes that represent your plan. Then put them on a board. Once that's done, hang it in your bedroom. I promise you'll be surprised at what a difference it makes.

Vision Board Components*

Images. By far the most common item to find on vision boards, images can be photos, drawings, mind maps, sketches or anything else that has some meaning for you.

Motivational messages. You've seen those motivation posters that say things such as, "Always believe that something wonder is about to happen." Or, "Some people miss the message because they are too busy looking for the mistake." For many, these messages can be extremely powerful. When you face a rough patch, simply remembering that phrase can be enough to get you back on track again.

Everything else. What else inspires or motivates you? The first tooth your child lost? A small vial of sand from that secluded beach you'll retire to someday? Your daughter's baby shoes? Vision boards can include these treasures as well; you just might have to be a little creative when it comes to adding them.

Have Fun With It

Remember when you were a kid in art class? Your vision board materials can be just as much fun—especially if you're creating a physical board to hang on your wall.

Start by gathering up a selection of materials to work with:

- A stack of old magazines (hit up your local library for their outdated copies)
- Colored pencils and markers
- Construction paper
- Poster board
- Glue and tape
- Scissors

Then begin to flip through the magazines. Resist the urge to get sucked into the articles, and instead, concentrate on how you feel as you see the photos. Do they make you happy? Do you smile at a particular shot? Does it suggest a particular goal or dream? Cut out the images that speak to you in some way.

Don't worry about organizing them or categorizing them at this point. For now, just make a stack of images that have meaning for you.

Next, take your board—and it can be a single piece of paper, a full-size poster board, or even the bulletin board in your office—and begin arranging your images, quotes and other materials.

You can have a single board with areas devoted to each aspect of your life, or a different board for each. Your board can be a hodgepodge of random images, or a carefully laid out plan that progresses naturally from one to the next. It can be color coordinated or not. Ultimately, it has to please no one but you, so let your creativity flow.

Don't be afraid to use your pencils and markers to decorate your board, draw attention to certain images, or divide it into distinct quadrants. You can add dates and dollar figures if you like, or the names of people you want to think of as you work with it.

Most importantly, just have fun.

Chapter Notes

An Invitation from April

Get started living the life you crave. Start coaching with me for even faster results. You're probably asking yourself: "Do I really need a Professional Coach?" The honest answer is no, you don't. But you also don't NEED a college degree. Nor do you NEED to possess killer organizational skills. But most people don't regret having either one. Just like a Professional Coach. But, often the additional perspective is invaluable.

A Certified Professional Coach assists clients in developing the strategy, motivation and accountability (their blueprint) required to succeed in their professional as well as their personal lives. Here are a few questions I can help you tackle:

- Is it time to evaluate your life?
- Are things going well?
- What's bothering you?
- What do you need or want to change?

Together we'll do a little self-evaluation. Then we'll discuss a personalized plan to make positive changes in your life. Finally, I'll oversee the implementation of these tactics so your transition to a path that helps you achieve your goals is a smooth one.

When we see an athlete accept an award, inevitably one of the persons thanked is their coach. Or coaches. That's because most athletes realize they would never reach their full potential without the help of a coach. You'd be surprised how many working professionals feel the same way. Eight-six percent of companies say they made more than their initial investment back when they used outside professional coaching.

Are you currently reaching the fullest extent of your potential? If not, then maybe you can benefit from a coach.

Although I do not work exclusively with either gender, I do specialize with women. I help businesswomen succeed in their professional as well as personal lives. To accomplish this, I have developed a 3-stage technique that I (and my clients) have had great success with. The 3 stages are:

- Develop a strategy.
- Build motivation.
- Create accountability (the business of you, if you will) required for success.

If you have any experience with coaching, you know one of the biggest keys to success is good chemistry between you and the coach. To help us get a head start on seeing if we gel, I'll give you what would be my answer to one of those questionnaires where they ask "What would your friends say about you?" I would say (meaning I think my friends would say):

> "I am independent, determined, analytical and deliberative. Sometimes I can be overly cautious, other times overly calculating. Some friends might label my sense of ethics as unshakable. I can sometimes be introverted. I am truthful, honest and sincere. I love my family and do everything I can to make sure they have what they need".

If you think you can work with someone like that, please, contact me. Better yet, to really see if we work, take advantage of a free coaching session offered. Visit my website to schedule an appointment today:

www.aprilbjones.com

Whether you decide to go on the journey alone or with a Professional Certified Coach, the first step is deciding to live the Life You Crave! Have the confidence to work toward becoming the next J.K. Rowling or Tyler Perry.

Connect With Me

- www.facebook.com/apribjonescoaching
- www.twitter.com/aprilbjones
- www.linkedin.com/in/aprilbjones
- www.instagram.com/aprilbjones

About the Author

April B. Jones is a Certified Professional Coach in Washington, D.C. Her mission is to assist clients in developing the strategy, motivation and accountability required to succeed in their professional and personal lives. Her knowledge of organizational leadership, human capital management and information management is supported by partnering with corporations, non-profit and charity organizations. She has over 20 years of experience with the U.S. Federal Government in management and information technology, more than ten years consulting experience with non-profit organizations and small business enterprises.

She is a member of the International Coach Federation, is certified by the Center for Coaching Certification as a Professional Coach, holds a double Master of Science Degree in Information Management with a specialization in Government from Syracuse University in Syracuse, New York and Telecommunication and Information Systems from Capitol College in Laurel, Maryland, has been recognized by Strathmore's Who's Who Global Network for Outstanding Professionals, received a Governor's Citation by the State of Maryland for her outstanding accomplishments and dedicated service, serves on the Chief Learning Officer Business Intelligence Board, the Professional Woman Network (PWN) International Board, the Board of Directors for the Berry Valley Homeowner Association, is a member of the National Association of Professional Women, and has also been featured in Black Enterprise and National Association of Female Executive magazines.

Ms. Jones is the co-author of Beyond the Body – Developing Inner Beauty (PWN 2007), The Young Man's Guide for Personal Success (PWN 2008), Learning to Love Yourself (PWN 2009), Life Skills for the African American Woman (PWN 2009), Raising African American Boys (PWN 2009), The Journey Within: Self-Discovery for Women (PWN

2009), Remove the Mask! How to Become Real and Live the Life You Want! (PWN 2009), The Woman's Handbook for Self-Empowerment – Lifting Women on a Global Basis (PWN 2009) and The Business of You – The Life You Crave (PWN 2017).

www.ingramcontent.com/pod-product-compliance
Lightning Source LLC
Chambersburg PA
CBHW071136090426
42736CB00012B/2130